SUCCESSFUL INVESTING

THROUGH MUTUAL FUNDS

Successful Investing
Through Mutual Funds

Robert Frank

With a foreword by Robert D. Hershey, Jr.

Hart Publishing Co., Inc., New York City

To my wife, the best capital gain of all

ACKNOWLEDGEMENTS

The author wishes to express his gratitude for the assistance, guidance and advice offered by Mr. Russ Idler, whose experience in investment counseling and mutual fund structure and operation has been of incalculable value. For his critical reading of the manuscript and for his helpful suggestions, I am deeply indebted.

Contents

Introduction   11

Foreword   15

1. What Is a Mutual Fund?   21

2. A Short History   27

3. Advantages of Investing in Mutual Funds   31

4. Investment Objectives   40

5. Who Rates the Funds and How?   54

6. The Record of Performance   65

7. How to Understand a Prospectus   77

8. The Acquisition Charge in Mutual Funds   99

9. The "No-Load" Funds   108

10. The "Go-Go" Funds   121

11. Mutual Fund Investment Plans   134

12. Mutual Fund Withdrawal Plans   144

13. Your Legal Protections   162

14. The Management Fee   173

15. Selecting Your Funds   184

16. Toward the Future   198

Appendix I. *Sources of Information on Mutual Funds*   205

Appendix II. *Books and Special Studies on Mutual Funds*   209

Appendix III. *Magazine Articles of Interest*   212

Index   219

Introduction

Mutual funds are the fastest-growing investment vehicle in the United States. Prior to 1940 there were fewer than 100 funds, with assets of about $500 million. By 1961 there were over 200 funds, with nearly 5 million shareholder accounts, owned by individuals and institutions, investing $38 billion. In early 1968 there were over 400 funds with about 8 million accounts whose total value was between $45 and $50 billion. By September, 1968, according to the Capital Gains Research Bureau, Inc., the aggregate assets of 191 funds (each with assets of more than $25 million) were $54 billion. The Bureau forecasts that fund assets will increase to more than $100 billion by 1975. Each day the number of investors grows and the capital assets of the more than 400 funds increase dramatically.

It has been estimated that within ten years the number of mutual fund investors will increase to 25 million. Hopefully, this book will help the thousands of investors on that continually expanding horizon, because as more and more people invest in mutual funds the need for their being well informed on the subject is crucial. Yet, too many investors feel that the subject, like Wall Street generally, is a kind of mystery religion; the high priest is the broker, the sacred scriptures are either dull financial tables or prospectuses written in

11

a foreign language, and an investor's economic salvation ultimately depends on a mercifully benevolent fate.

First, the ABC's of mutual funds have been written about very superficially in slim hard-sell pamphlets put out by brokerage houses, in columns by some well-known financial writers in metropolitan dailies, and in magazine articles or brief stories in news-weeklies.

Second, there are monthly magazines that analyze and rate fund performance in many categories, contain articles of special interest on mutual funds, and publish an annual mutual fund directory. Then there is a bi-monthly magazine that devotes a column to the funds and annually rates fund performance. There are also highly specialized companies that publish annual supplements to their basic books on mutual funds. A major fund industry spokesman publishes articles and books on funds. Also available are detailed, technical studies prepared for the government. All these publications are excellent; however, they are caviar for the sophisticated, the investors who have some knowledge of the field, the "advanced students" as it were.

Third, there are books that take a dogmatic, categorical position on mutual funds. Aside from their heavily biased views as obstacles to clear understanding, these books also assume a degree of knowledge and experience that mark only a limited number of readers. In the hands of the inexperienced, such books can be very misleading.

Finally, there are books that take an informal approach to the funds. They try to meet the novice on his own ground. One of the most popular of these was written by a man with strong ties to the mutual fund industry. Another was prepared for the fund industry itself, to be used, possibly, by brokers.

My book attempts to bring mutual funds much closer to the neophyte, to anticipate his questions and to answer them simply and informally. For when it comes to talking about their money, people are rarely insulted by simplicity and clarity. It is for those who want to invest in mutual funds or who think they do but . . . It is also for those already in funds who really may not understand too much of what it is all about. My premise is that any fund investor, actual or potential, wants a book that will help him

—to understand what is undoubtedly one of the greatest investment opportunities of the mid-twentieth century.
—to recognize why mutual funds will probably be the leading investment that millions of Americans will make in the next 10 years.
—to make intelligent decisions about whether to invest in mutual funds and how to invest.
—to remain unvictimized, unterrorized and unperturbed.

To achieve these goals you need not be an expert. You need only be well informed, observant, curious, and reasonably intelligent, willing to take some time to study and to plan. This is no more than the kind of commonsense-approach many Americans take before buying a house or a car or an insurance policy.

The mutual fund industry is well established; it is in many respects tightly regulated to protect citizens; its virtues are almost universally acknowledged; its weaknesses are variously identified or disagreed about, depending on the critic. My book will not help you "get rich quick" or "speculate" in mutual funds. As will become clear, it is exceedingly difficult for an ordinary citizen to "speculate" in mutual funds although it is true that some mutual funds are more speculative than others.

I am not associated with any brokerage house, mutual fund, or sales staff for any investment organization. I am associated only with you, the reader, who is apparently eager to learn about mutual funds and to put to work what you learn. If so, the chances are good that you can protect your money against shrinkage while it is working for you and your future. *If,* that is, you are willing to invest in the economic future of the United States.

Foreword

*Behold, the fool saieth, "Put not all thine eggs in the one basket"—which is but a manner of saying, "Scatter your money and your attention"; but the wise man saieth, "Put all your eggs in the one basket and—*WATCH THAT BASKET!

Mark Twain

The modern mutual fund is probably the best financial basket ever offered investors. It combines *professional* money management—certainly a more successful method than that of amateurs—with the best features of both concentration and diversification. It is conveniently packaged, advertised for what it is—though often misunderstood—and marvelously efficient. It is honestly run.

The fund is the ideal vehicle for serious investors, both large and small, whose goal is making capital increase in value over long periods. The concept is simply unassailable.

A proper investment in a mutual fund is above all a commitment to a financial strategy—one, however, that is extremely difficult for many individuals to make. Purchasers of funds give up something that, though financially worthless, is of enormous psychic value to market dabblers—the pleasure of exchanging gossip with friends. They take, in effect, a pledge to forego cocktail-party profundities like "The steels look pretty good" or "I'm short I.B.M.—it's way

15

overpriced." They have decided that given the choice between fun and profit, they'll take profit.

Some persons, of course, invest both in funds and in individual stocks. But the wise ones, for the most part, kid themselves about their sagacity in calling market turns or in selecting securities.

This, of course, does not mean that fund managers are necessarily smarter than other mortals. Far from it. But they are professionals—men devoting *full time* to their business. This well outweighs any advantage of maneuverability an individual might have.

There are men who trade stocks on their own for large, quick, profits. But it can't be done by factory workers and doctors in their spare time: SPECULATION IS A FULL-TIME OCCUPATION.

The mutual fund business, less than 50 years old in this country, is booming. Over 400 funds hold a total of $50 billion, compared with $2 billion in 1940; 64 new funds were marketed during 1968; nearly 100 more, if closed-end investment companies are included, are now awaiting clearance from the Securities and Exchange Commission. What's more, the life insurance industry has recently invaded the field, a step of such significance that its eventual impact can only be wildly estimated.

Such public demand for a product naturally inspires competition, proliferation, innovation, sometimes even gimmickry. This is why Robert Frank's *Successful Investing Through Mutual Funds* is so valuable. Taking nothing for granted, he explains in some detail —yet clearly—how funds operate, what types there are, and how to select them to meet various objectives.

The book has been written with the neophyte in mind, but there is substantial material that existing fund-holders—not always as well-informed as they believe—will find informative.

From the point of view of a reporter on the mutual fund beat, one of Mr. Frank's most important points is this: "The biggest mistake a mutual fund investor can make is to assess a fund's performance in terms of a brief period like three months, or six months, or a year."

Scarcely a day passes that I do not receive telephone calls or letters asking for the address of a fund that only a few dozen people have ever heard of. Such inquiries come from somebody who has seen or heard statistics showing that the fund performed well in the latest period.

This is difficult information for me to come up with. The hottest fund changes every day; they are almost always too new to be listed in reference books or trade magazines.

The rise of this performance cult is changing the face of the business and is the most likely source of investor grief. Many persons, both inside and outside the industry, believe that the most aggressive funds are taking excessive risks in their quest for high profits.

There's no doubt that these funds have a place. The danger is that many of the wrong people are buying them with false expectations. Mutual funds, as Mr. Frank makes abundantly clear, are not today the automatically stolid, safe investments they all were considered to be until the 1960's.

On a separate matter, on which Mr. Frank touches only to the extent necessary for his purposes, it seems to me vital that potential mutual fund investors not be distracted by the controversy surrounding government and government-sponsored reports critical of the industry.

Much of the criticism is quite persuasive. But the issues are not those that should scare off prospective investors. The industry is not crooked, its managers are not incompetent, and promises are not unfulfilled. Nobody has made *such* charges.

The Securities and Exchange Commission, perhaps the severest critic, declared in its famous 1966 study of the PUBLIC POLICY IMPLICATIONS OF INVESTMENT COMPANY GROWTH:

"The Commission finds that on the whole the investment company industry reflects diligent management by competent persons. . . . The investment company industry has acted responsibly to provide a useful and desirable means for investors to obtain diversification of investment risks and professional investment management."

Whether sales charges and management fees should be reduced, or whether installment purchases of funds should be abolished is something that the Congress will decide. While it deliberates, however, investors should keep things in perspective. The key to successful investing on the part of nonprofessionals is mutual funds. It is a strategy that will easily overcome the few extra dollars of expense in acquiring shares and involves paying a small fraction of a percent additional for the cost of professional management.

These extra costs are only tiny leaks—from the investor's standpoint—in a large basket that in all likelihood will hold a bountiful harvest over the years.

ROBERT D. HERSHEY, JR.
Financial-Business News Reporter
The New York Times

SUCCESSFUL INVESTING

THROUGH MUTUAL FUNDS

1   What Is a Mutual Fund?

Early in 1967 a friend of mine, a civil engineer, prepared for the ordeal of his April income tax by consulting an accountant for the first time. A man of modest means, he learned of many legitimate savings he could have made in the years when he had prepared his own tax return. He also learned some grim truths.

The accountant first pointed out that the modest dividend of 5% a year on an account with a credit union or a savings account was subject in full to income tax. Then he showed that although my friend's savings had been drawing 5% yearly interest, the purchasing power of the principal was less than it had been five years earlier. Finally, he proved that if accelerated inflation continued on top of normal inflation the value of the savings in 1973 would be a little more than half of what it was in 1963.

He suggested that if my friend were to keep a few thousand dollars for emergency and were to invest what was left, he might receive a tax break and also protect his incredibly shrinking savings. He referred him to an investment broker. Two months later my friend invested $5,000 in two mutual funds.

This past March, twelve months later, his investment was worth $5,900 or an increase of 18%. While the value of his investment will fluctuate, it will undoubtedly hold to an "up pattern" if the history of mutual funds and the growth of the United States economy are any criteria. One thing is sure: for the first time in his life he has protection—not a guarantee but protection—against the decreasing purchasing power of his savings. He has realized that there is no opportunity without risk and that guarantees can prevent opportunity.

There are thousands of people like him who have permitted their money to lie year after year with the principal drawing interest but the total value shriveling. Such a sorry past could be prelude to a brighter future, however, simply by an investment in mutual funds.

A Mutual Fund

A mutual fund is a pooling of money by a group of investors. They select a professional manager who invests their money in a variety of stocks, bonds, and other securities that he believes will earn dividends and profits. These are then distributed to each investor in proportion to the amount of money each has put into the pool.

To see how it works, let us imagine a small group, say 100 people. Each contributes $10 to a pool for a total of $1,000. Each member owns one share. Not knowing very much about the quality or the kinds of stocks and bonds, they hire a manager for a fee of ⅛ of 1% per quarter, or ½ of 1% of the fund's assets *as of the end of the year*. Each then goes about his business.

One year later the manager calls them together and reports as follows:

"I am happy to tell you that the stocks and bonds that I purchased have appreciated in value. I bought shares in the stocks of five companies. The total value of the shares is now $1,200. In addition, three companies declared dividends this year. The total dividends that our shares in those companies earned was $100. Furthermore, five months ago I sold one stock for $200 more than

I paid for it and replaced it with another. Your original $1,000 is now worth

a. Value of the stocks we hold: $1,200
b. Dividends from the stocks: 100
c. Profit from sale of stock: 200
                                   _____
                                     $1,500

Deducting my management fee of ½ of 1% or $7.50 leaves $1,492.50. Each of you owns one share and there are 100 shares outstanding, so each share is worth $14.925. Each of you has a profit of 49¼%."

This group must now make an important decision. Some of their friends and associates would like to buy shares in the group. Should the group qualify the fund as an "open-end" investment company and guarantee the redemption of shares by the fund? Or should they qualify the fund as a "closed-end" investment company and allow the shares to be traded as are other stock issues in the "over-the-counter" market? Either way, the group may do so well that some day each share could have an asset value of $100.

If the group decides to "open" their fund, it will be known as an "open-end investment company" or a "mutual fund." If the group decides to issue no more shares, it will be called a "closed-end investment company."

Note the following key terms and meanings as applied to mutual funds:

1. *Net Asset Value Per Share.* This is determined by dividing the total value of the fund's holdings in stocks, bonds, securities and cash by the number of shares outstanding. For most funds it is computed once daily.

2. *Portfolio.* This is the variety of stocks and bonds in which a fund has invested. During a year there may be few additions

and deletions or there may be many. The management decides what will be traded and when, to accomplish the investment objective that it has selected.

3. *Volatility.* This describes the trading frequency of securities held in the fund portfolio. The greater the volatility, the greater the expense incurred by the fund in the way of commissions.

4. *Management Fee.* This is the fee, usually ½ of 1% of the fund's total assets, which is charged by the manager of the fund. The fee is deducted *before* the net asset value of a share is calculated (annually or quarterly) for dividend purposes. The fee is *not* deducted in the daily computation of the net asset value per share.

5. *Dividends from Investments.* Usually stated in *per share* terms, these are the total of all the dividends and interest paid by stocks and bonds held in a fund's portfolio divided by the total number of outstanding shares in the fund. For example, if Fund A with 10,000 shares outstanding has $1,000,000 invested in 30 stocks and those stocks paid dividends totaling $2,500, the per share dividend in the mutual fund will be $.25. Most funds distribute per share dividends annually. Some distribute them quarterly.

6. *Capital Gain.* This is the profit made on the trading of stocks and bonds. For example, during the year if Fund A sells one of its stock holdings for $2,500 more than it cost, that is a capital gain. With 10,000 shares outstanding in the fund, that will be a $.25 capital gain distribution per share. Most funds distribute capital gains to their shareholders once a year.

In summary, then, when you buy a share in a mutual fund you are pooling your money with others to acquire an interest in a broad variety of stocks and bonds. As the companies grow and make profits, and as the securities yield returns, your mutual fund shares earn *dividends* and *capital gains,* and the net assets of the fund increase. All this increases the value of a share in the fund. You can take your dividends and capital gains in cash or you can choose to have them *reinvested* in the fund to acquire more shares.

Let us briefly return to our small group and imagine that they have now existed for five years. Our fund has total net assets of $89,135,221. There are 30,151 shareholders who own a total of 5,410.040 shares with a net asset value of $16.48 a share. This year's annual dividend was $.23 per share and capital gains distributions were $1.09 per share *after all operating costs and the management fee were deducted.* The fund's portfolio of securities consists of 86% common stocks (of 69 different companies, in blocks of 5,000 or more shares) 0.2% preferred stock, 0.9% corporate bonds, 0.5% U.S. Treasury Notes, and 12.4% short-term commercial notes.

One very important new factor is present: there are many other successful funds competing with ours. The management of our fund has hired brokers to sell shares in our fund at a sales charge of 9% of the net asset value of $16.48 a share. So, if a newcomer invests $100 in our fund, $91 of it will go to buy shares and $9 will go for sales charges. Other funds that hire no brokers of their own rely on independent dealers who hire brokers to sell their fund shares, the price of which includes a sales charge up to 9%. Some brokers handle only certain funds, others sell almost all the funds.

This sales charge is part of the cost of a share in most funds. It is called the "load charge" and ranges from 1% to 9%. Most mutual funds today are load funds. Funds whose shares can be bought without any sales charge are called "no-load" funds. Load and no-load funds raise a number of obviously important questions and are dealt with in Chapters 8 and 9.

Let us call our fund the "Advocate Fund." It is now large

enough to be listed in most big metropolitan newspapers, usually under the heading "Investment Trusts" or "Mutual Funds" or "Investment Funds." Here is a sample of how our fund would be listed among a dozen funds in a typical daily listing. In the right-hand column is an explanation of the difference between the two figures "Bid" and "Ask."

INVESTMENT TRUSTS

New York (AP)
—The following quotations, supplied by the National Association of Securities Dealers, Inc., are the prices at which these securities could have been sold (bid) or bought (asked) Friday:

	Bid	Ask
Abalone	$ 3.19	$ 3.49
Administrators	8.76	9.59
Advocate	16.48	17.88
Affluent	9.14	9.89
Alamo	1.23	1.34
Amcorp	6.26	6.84
Amarind	3.67	3.97
Amspace	11.52	12.59
Antique	8.09	8.79
Appropriate	10.02	10.02
Aquanaut	10.37	11.33
Astronomers	7.75	7.75

The difference between the "bid" and "ask" figures is the sales charge. One share of Advocate would cost you $17.88. That includes an 8½% sales charge which comes to $1.40 a share. If you wished to sell your share of Advocate immediately after purchasing it, it would be worth $16.48.

Eight and a half percent is the usual sales charge although most funds decrease it as the size of the investment increases.

When the "bid" and "ask" figures are identical, you know that the fund is a "no-load" fund.

2   A Short History

Mutual funds were virtually unknown in 1940. Up to that time, particularly in the 1920's, the commonest kind of fund was the "closed-end" investment trust briefly described on page 23. Like many investment groups in the 1920's, these were flying high. Management fees were exorbitant. Commission splitting was legion. With huge concentrations of cash at their disposal, managers invested readily in all kinds of wildcat, speculative stock issues that were practically worthless, many times promising the investor quick, large profits. They bought on margin (buying a stock by just making a low down payment) and invaded whole industries with cash that came from the investor. Paper profits piled high; interlocking directorates and controls mushroomed.

When the stock market exploded in 1929 there were over 600 investment trusts claiming assets of $6 to $7 billion. The crash showed many "wealthy" trusts to be practically worthless. It was to protect the public against these excesses that the Securities and Exchange Commission began a detailed study of the investment trusts industry in the mid-1930's. The fruit of the SEC's work appeared in the Investment Company Act of 1940 which represented a milestone in legislation that would protect the public from the nefarious

27

trust practices of the 1920's. It should be noted that while many closed-end trusts went bankrupt during this period, not one open-end trust (mutual fund) folded.

The Commission issued a new charter for the closed-end trusts and for open-end trusts, setting strict standards for organization, collateral, open disclosure of assets, submission of prospectuses, load charges, management fees, and advertising. Fund managers wanted the right to advertise their wares, but since open-end funds constantly issue new shares of stock, they had to abide by the Investment Company Act of 1933. This Act required that fund advertising be limited to the name of the fund, the offering of a prospectus, and a brief description of the fund's objectives.

Since 1940 the funds have grown fantastically. The net asset value of the entire industry was about half a billion dollars in 1940. By 1960 it was $20 billion, by 1966 over $40 billion, and by 1968 it was close to $50 billion, with at least half a dozen funds having assets exceeding $1 billion.

In recent years the funds have been rocked by two major developments. One is the government's insistence that "front-end load" be outlawed; the second is the claim that the sales charge or load is excessive and ought to be significantly reduced. What are front-end load funds? Under a front-end load plan (often called a "contractual plan") a buyer agrees to invest a specific amount of money in a fund over a stated period of time, usually ten or twelve years. Up to 50% of the investor's total payments in the first year may legally go toward the sales charge which includes the broker's commission and other sales expenses. Pending legislation may change this sales charge to 20% of the first year's investment. Signing up for a $50-a-month plan, the customer pays $600 the first year, $300 of which can legally be taken for the sales charge.

The advantage is all to the dealer and his brokers: they get most of their total commission due over the life of the contract in the first year. Many brokers agree that the front-end load is *not* in the investor's best interest. Some industry executives argue that a front-end load is an incentive to an investor to save systematically, but critics argue that it is an unconscionable burden on an investor. There is every indication that the SEC will agree to a 20% front-end load. "Contractual plans" are outlawed in some states, California among them.

The second major change called for in mutual funds by the SEC was the reduction of the sales charge to 5%. This jolted the industry and stirred much acrimonious debate. Arguments for, and criticisms of, load charges are considered in Chapter 8.

In 1968 the SEC was also reviewing management fees. The ½ of 1% does not sound like much, but when you consider that in a fund of $250,000,000 the fee would be $1,250,000, you get some idea of the money involved. The management fee dispute is examined in detail in Chapter 14.

In June, 1968, the Senate Banking Committee approved legislation dealing with these three controversial issues in the following ways:

1. Front-end load charges on contractual plans were limited to 20% in any one year and a cumulative total of 64% over the first four years.

2. Sales charges on open ("Voluntary") accounts were left up to industry self-regulation through the National Association of Securities Dealers, but the final power was given to the SEC to fix them if it disagrees with the industry's determination.

3. Management fees were left alone, subject to SEC scrutiny through its power to file court cases to determine the fee's reasonableness; however, the courts would be directed to consider the action of unaffiliated directors of a fund in approving the fees.

The second and third items constituted some kind of victory for the funds, but the extent and the degree to which the industry's self-regulation will occur remain to be seen. Equally interesting will be the reaction of the SEC. The industry is bitter over the prospect of having to reduce sales charges. Its spokesmen, as well as a legion of brokerage houses, insist that the mutual fund industry has grown largely because of the sales charge incentive. While undoubtedly true, this is only part of the story. Mutual funds have also grown because they are, in certain respects, excellent investments with many elements of appeal. Furthermore, there is a wide variety of types of mutual funds (discussed in Chapter 15) from which the most conservative or the most speculative investor can choose.

Easily the most significant development in the proliferation of funds and fund assets in 1967 and 1968 has been the entry into the field by huge organizations such as insurance companies. Life insurance policyowners are borrowing on or cashing in their life insurance policies in large numbers. The life insurance companies obviously want this money for their own investments but cannot reverse the trend. So, for the purpose of investing the cash value, many life insurance companies have begun offering funds as a part of their program.

The future of the fund industry is apparently wide open. One fund at the end of April, 1968, had assets of $1.5 million. Thirty days later it had assets of over $6 million. Another fund in March, 1968, had $2 million in assets. Sixty days later it had $25,000,000 in assets. A third fund in mid-1967 had assets of $89,000,000. By mid-1968 its assets had grown to $561 million! Such phenomenal growth should not be considered as representative but is cited here for purposes of illustration.

The future of the mutual fund industry will be anything but dull! The following chapters will help you to take advantage of your opportunity to get acquainted with this fascinating investment medium.

3 Advantages of Investing in Mutual Funds

Everyone knows "how the prices of things have gone up." Whether it is a pack of cigarettes a year ago, a loaf of bread two years ago, or a can of beans three years ago, a day rarely passes without some reminder of how much costs have risen. Like the weather and taxes, increased prices are what you think you can do nothing about. You are only partially right.

While you cannot prevent rising prices, you can try to protect yourself against the decline in the purchasing power of your dollar. You can invest your dollars so that you will accumulate a greater number of them over an extended period of time than you would if you were to let them lie in a savings account and accumulate only a *fixed* additional number each year while they continue declining in value. A savings account is like a rest home for your money while your investment of those dollars in mutual funds puts them to work.

1. *Investing in mutual funds presents an opportunity to protect yourself against inflation-shrinking dollars.* You may be unaware of the toll of inflation over an extended period, say five to ten years. While you lament a price rise over the last year on a particular household article, your blood pressure might really rise if you

viewed the effects of inflation over a longer period of time. For example, suppose you had taken $1,000 on January 1, 1948, and buried it in the ground. Digging it up on December 31, 1967, you'll find that you could have bought $720 worth of goods with it. In other words, had you put aside a lump sum toward retirement in 1948, 20 years later it would have been worth less than ¾ of what you started with! As the figures get larger, of course, the story gets sadder.

Now suppose that you had taken that $1,000 on January 1, 1948, and considered (a) putting it in the ground; (b) buying a Series "E" Government Bond; (c) putting it in a savings account; or (d) putting it into a reputable mutual fund whose growth prospects were good, based on past performance and the expectation of a healthy economy.

The table below covers the period from January 1, 1948, to December 31, 1967. It compares an assumed investment in the shares of a well-known fund with investments having a *fixed return* for the same period. The comparison shows the differences among contrasting ways of investing. The results in government bonds are guaranteed. The principal in a savings bank is also guaranteed. Results in the fund are not guaranteed and cannot be predicted in advance because the fund's value fluctuates and the dividends vary in amount from year to year.

The period was one of generally rising common stock prices and the results of an investment in the mutual fund shares should be measured in the light of the fund's policies and objectives—in this case, capital growth.

A sales charge of 7½% per share in the mutual fund has been used in this calculation.

Footnote number 4 needs stressing. Capital gains distributions were not taken in cash but were used, at the investor's specific instructions, to purchase as many shares as possible at the time of

	Amount Invested 1–1–48	Investment Income Received	Total	Asset Value 12–31–67	Purchasing Power[1] 12–31–67
Cash	$1,000		$1,000	$1,000	$ 720
Govt. Bonds, Series E	1,000	$ 886	1,886	1,886[2]	1,358
4% Savings Acct.	1,000	1,208	2,208	2,208[3]	1,589
5% Savings Acct.	1,000	1,685	2,685	2,685[3]	1,933
6% Savings Acct.	1,000	2,262	3,262	3,262[3]	2,348
Mutual Fund	1,000	2,395	3,395	8,446[4]	6,081

[1] According to figures prepared by the Bureau of Labor Statistics, the 1967 dollar bought only 72.0% as much as the 1948 dollar.
[2] Compound interest at 2.9% until May, 1952, then 3.0% until February, 1957, then 3.25% until June, 1959, then 3.75% to December, 1965, and then 4.15% to December 31, 1967.
[3] Interest compounded semiannually.
[4] Includes reinvestment of $2,861 realized capital gains.

each distribution. Note, also, that dividends were taken in cash: had they, too, been reinvested in more shares, the asset value of the fund holding would have been even greater.

If you really want an eye-opener, multiply each figure by 10. Ten thousand dollars in cash after 20 years was $10,000 in asset value and $7,200 in purchasing power; $10,000 in the mutual fund after 20 years had an asset value of $84,468 and a purchasing power of $60,817! Again, it must be pointed out that there is no guarantee that this performance will be repeated.

2. *Investing in a mutual fund enables you to diversify your investment in a broad spectrum of stocks and bonds.* If you had $1,000 to invest, you could buy 100 shares at $10 a share in only one company. If the stock dropped, you would lose substantially. If it rose, you would gain substantially. But suppose you bought $1,000 worth of different stocks? You have cushioned yourself against extreme loss, you have enhanced your chances of a healthy gain and you have decided to take a middle-of-the-road expectation

of a significant gain if the American economy remains healthy. Furthermore, you are actually much closer to the economy with investment in 10 companies than in only one.

3. *Investing in a mutual fund may significantly reduce your investment risks.*

A.   The first reduced risk is one already mentioned, the one against severe loss that you might incur if all your money was in one stock. It should be noted that mutual funds have the same potential for loss that they have for growth; however, all things considered, you are better off because of the professional management that you obtain through fund ownership.

B.   The second risk that you minimize is one that you are probably very self-conscious about: faulty judgments because of your inexperience. While the manager of a fund is obviously interested in his fee, his primary motive is to make money for you, the shareholder, so that you will continue investing and so that new investors will invest in the fund. The manager has a great deal of knowledge and experience for which you are paying a yearly fee of ½ of 1% of the net asset value of your shares. Unlike some brokers, fund management does not advise you, it does not pressure you to buy, it does not take advantage of your inexperience. It gives you, instead, performance that reflects its continual use of its experience and skill. Management increases, decreases, or holds the fund's portfolio investments in view of daily developments in our economy. Management, then, is constantly making decisions about how to use your money in order to make more money for you.

A further safeguard against your lack of experience may be the broker whose commission of 3% to 4% buys you advice about where to put your money. Ultimately, the decision is yours, but the broker's commission is supposed to compensate him for his overhead, his research, training, experience, counsel, and time.

C.   A third risk that you diminish in mutual fund investing is the amount of your loss in declining market periods. The *rate of decline* in the value of a fund during depressed periods is sometimes not revealed by an eager broker who wants you to buy into the fund; yet, such decline periods are a fact of life in our economy. The record of the average mutual fund in declining markets is good. Two notable periods of declining stock values were December 31, 1961, to June 28, 1962, and February 9, 1966, to October 7, 1966. The average decline in the net asset value of mutual fund shares in those periods, using data compiled by *FundScope* from 260 funds, was 21.5% and 19.6% respectively. Incidentally, during the first period, the widely used Dow Jones Industrial Average was down 23.7% (21.6% when adjusted for dividends paid) and during the second period it was down 25.2% (22.6% when adjusted for dividends paid).

4. *Investing in mutual funds provides an opportunity for "dollar-cost averaging."* This is not a unique advantage in mutual fund investing but it has great appeal if you have only a limited (but definite) amount of money to invest regularly. A number of funds accept as little as $25.00 initially and $25.00 per month thereafter. When you use "dollar-cost averaging" you buy fewer shares when prices are high and more shares when prices are low. In the long run, you get a better-than-average price per share.

Assume that you plan to invest $100 monthly. Also assume that

Month	Investment	Sales Charge	Amount Invested	Asset Value	Shares Purchased
Jan.	$100	$8.50	$91.50	$ 8.00	11.437
Feb.	100	8.50	91.50	10.00	9.150
March	100	8.50	91.50	9.00	10.166
April	100	8.50	91.50	8.00	11.437
May	100	8.50	91.50	7.50	12.466
June	100	8.50	91.50	8.00	11.437
	$600	$51.00	$549.00		66.093

the sales charge is 8½ %. The preceding table indicates how dollar-cost averaging could work for you. Fractional shares are shown here.

Dividing the $549 actually invested by the fund by the 66 shares that you own, you find that the shares have cost you an average of $8.31 per share. Over a relatively long period of time, the "average" cost of shares that you purchase will probably be significantly lower than their liquidation value.

5. *Investing in mutual funds is a great bookkeeping convenience.*   The time and bother of keeping a record of dividend payments, profit or loss on securities, and the handling of certificates of ownership is reduced to a minimum. Depending on the fund, quarterly, semiannual, or annual reports are mailed to the shareholder, with comments on the fund's performance and detailed financial statements giving the asset value of the shares, a list of the securities owned, and other pertinent information. A shareholder in a mutual fund cannot easily claim that he is in the dark. State and Federal laws are strict in their requirements for full disclosure of the fund's financial condition.

6. *Investing in a mutual fund offers a special advantage to the self-employed and their employees.*   The "Self-Employed Individual's Tax Retirement Act of 1962" (also known as the "Keogh Act" and "HR-10") provided that you could invest up to $1,250 a year (amended in 1966 to $2,500 a year) in a mutual fund with the total amount deductible for income tax purposes. Until you retire, you do not have to pay any income tax on any dividends or capital gains distributions paid into the account, nor may these assets be attached or divided under community property laws. The tax deductibility feature makes a Keogh plan an attractive retirement vehicle.

7. *Investing in a mutual fund is an excellent way to build a retirement account from which you can make regular withdrawals.* In times of growth and stability in our economy, you may finish each year with a greater amount of capital in your fund holdings than when you started, depending upon the rate and type of withdrawal. Most funds have systematic withdrawal plans. They sometimes require either an initial or an accumulated investment of $10,000, although some have no minimum. Withdrawals of $50 a month or more (the usual recommendation is 6% a year) are permitted.

Such plans do not, and cannot, insure a profit, nor do they protect you against loss in declining market periods. Obviously, payments to you may exceed dividends and capital gains distributions paid on your shares. To that extent your capital in the fund will be reduced. For a closer look at various withdrawal plans in typical funds and how they might work out for representative investors and various amounts of capital, see Chapter 12.

Caution!

Although there are distinct advantages in mutual fund investing, there are also other realities that must not be forgotten. These realities may conflict sharply with your expectations if you are inexperienced. Some of the factors that tend to obscure certain basic truths about mutual funds are the spectacular growth of funds, a few glamorous successes and the sense of personal involvement in "Wall Street."

1. *No rate of return on an investment in mutual funds can be guaranteed.* This is an elementary truth about equity investments. Viewed from the vantage point of a "guaranteed" return in a savings account, credit union, or bond, one may call the "no-guarantee" feature of mutual funds a "disadvantage." But one can

hardly argue with another elementary truth: that a fixed rate of return is never guaranteed to be accompanied by an increase in the purchasing power of that fixed return. There is no opportunity without risk.

You must ultimately decide for yourself whether the "no-guarantee" of a fund investment is a greater risk than the near certainty that inflation will eventually wipe out the purchasing power of a "guaranteed" investment. One fact is undeniable: in the past 20 years the United States' economy has generally been a growing, productive one, with the future even more promising. As you are well aware, however, in the past 20 years the dollar's purchasing power has steadily shriveled.

2. *Mutual funds are generally conservative and afford neither spectacular results nor quick profits.* Notions to the contrary may be traced to visions of the "market" as synonymous with a "quick buck." This fallacy is known to most Americans who remember the fiascos of the 1920's, the terrible crash of 1929, and the depression. The 1929 "get-rich-quick" dream of many individuals foolishly trading on a 10% margin nevertheless seeps unconsciously into the thinking of investors who expect royal, handsome, and immediate returns. It must be remembered, too, that many people today invest in mutual funds with an ardor that is uncooled by any vivid memories of a depression. Despite the cautionary words of a broker, you may find it difficult to forego your optimistic eagerness. Only time will reduce your great expectations and calm your excitement as you scan the net asset value per share of your fund in the newspaper.

3. *Mutual funds are not for trading.* There is, nevertheless, the common opinion that when one buys or sells or switches funds, he is making investment decisions comparable to trading in stocks. This is wrong.

By its nature (particularly the cost of investing), a mutual fund is not designed for trading but for long-term investing. It is true that different funds perform differently at particular times, but the actual net asset value of a share in the fund at any particular time reflects gains that it has already made up to that time. If one really wanted to turn a profit by trading in mutual funds, he would need to know *in advance* just what the manager of the fund intended investing in. He would also need to know how his investment was going to do before he could start profit trading. If he had a crystal ball that would do all this, what would he need with professional management?

Compare these "unknowns" for the mutual fund holder with the possible "knowns" for the investor in a particular stock of a particular corporation. The latter might know that the management changed three months ago and that the change has been accompanied by a 50% increase in the corporation's sales. He might know that 500 new employees had been added to the company and that five new branch offices were going to be opened throughout the country. That kind of information would encourage him to buy stock in the corporation, hold it for a brief period and then sell or trade it at a profit.

The mutual fund holder is twice-removed from these "knowns." If he attempts to do any trading at all, what he is trading in is not individual stocks but in the judgment, skill, and experience of individual fund managers. A fund is a long-term investment most often acquired over a long period. The errors in a man's fund investment have little to do with his trading ability. They have much to do with his errors of judgment in his initial selection of a fund. Investigate before you invest! It is easier to laugh about a poor decision that you almost made than to laugh about one that you have actually made.

4   Investment Objectives

Most mutual funds are long-term investments seeking one or more of three major purposes: *growth, income,* and *price stability.* An unusual fund may achieve all three purposes but each fund has one primary goal on which the manager of the fund will base his investment policy.

Growth

Probably one-half to three-quarters of all investors have growth of invested capital as their primary objective, therefore the great majority of funds are geared to that. "The purpose of the fund is to seek growth of invested capital" and "The purpose of this fund is to provide professional management for the resources of investors interested in long-term capital appreciation" are quotations from the objectives in the prospectuses of two representative funds.

How can your investment grow in a mutual fund? First, it can grow through an increase in the number of your shares, either through your periodic purchases or through your dividends and capital gains distributions being automatically reinvested to purchase new shares.

Increase in Shares through Periodic Purchases

Most funds provide plans for periodic purchases to suit your convenience and your budget. They are usually voluntary "open account," the only stipulation being some minimum investment starting as low as $10 and ranging up to $500 or some minimum number of shares. It varies greatly. One of the major advantages of periodic purchases is that they enable you to "dollar-cost average" (see pages 35–36).

Increase in Shares through Automatic Reinvestments

Growth funds usually recommend that you have your dividends and capital gains distributions automatically reinvested by the fund to purchase additional shares for your account. The fund will automatically handle all the details and arrangements if this is your choice.

When you study the history of a fund's performance for a hypothetical investment, note three figures: (1) the value of the investment if you had accepted the dividends and the capital gains distributions in cash; (2) the value of the investment if you had accepted the dividends in cash but had reinvested the capital gains distributions to purchase more shares; (3) the value of the investment if you had accepted all dividends and capital gains distributions in additional shares.

Suppose you had invested $1,000 in a well-known growth fund on January 1, 1958, and held it for ten years until December 31, 1967. Total cash dividends in your pocket would have been $279. Total capital gains distributions in your pocket would have been $990. And the value of the shares originally acquired would have been $2,567.

Suppose for the same investment you took only the dividends in cash but reinvested the capital gains distributions to purchase new shares. Cash in your pocket would have been $279. The capital gains distributions accepted as shares would have had a cumulative value of $1,389 (contrast that with the cash in pocket value of $990) added to the value of the shares originally acquired, $2,567, for a total liquidation value of $3,956 at the end of the ten-year period.

Finally, suppose you took all dividends and all capital gains distributions in additional shares. The total cumulative liquidation value of your investment would have been $4,478 at the end of the ten-year period. Compare this with $1,000 deposited in a savings account for ten years, drawing 5% interest compounded quarterly. After ten years it would be worth exactly $1,643.60 (see Compound Interest Chart, page 45).

Multiply all the above figures by five or ten to see how you would have done with an initial investment of $5,000 or $10,000, respectively. There is no guarantee that such results will be or can be repeated. The above example used $1,000 advisedly. Most growth funds, in the brochure that they will send you accompanying their prospectus, will usually use what they call "an assumed initial investment of $10,000." In a colorful chart they will show you the growth of the investment over the entire past life of the fund (sometimes 20 years) or over ten or 15 years. It is very impressive and very accurate but it has one weakness: it is somewhat unrealistic because many people cannot afford such a large initial investment.

When you see in a fund brochure such figures as "initial investment," "dividends," "capital gains distributions," "value of investment after ten years," etc., divide them by whatever fraction of the initial investment *you* could have made. That will give you an idea of how you would have done. Some funds also provide an analysis of an assumed investment of $50 or $100 per month over the same period.

Increase in a Share's Value by Profitable Investment

The second way in which your investment can grow is through an increase in the value of a share. The fund manager may invest in a portfolio of stocks and bonds whose value goes up and he may make capital gains from selling portfolio holdings at a profit.

Managers of growth funds invest your money primarily in "growth stocks." Here is one definition of a growth stock by the manager of a well-known fund:

" 'Growth stock' is a term used by many people with various meanings. The management of this fund defines a growth stock as a share in a business enterprise which has demonstrated long-term growth of earnings which may reach a new high level per share at the peak of each succeeding major business cycle and which gives indications for reaching new high earnings at the peak of future business cycles. Earnings growth per share should be at a faster rate than the rise in the cost of living. This will offset the dollar's loss of purchasing power.

"Even though the long-term trend is upward, the earnings and market values of growth stocks experience cyclical declines just like other common stocks during periods of business adversity.

"There is no mathematical formula that can be used to identify growth stocks. The requirements are a matter of judgment and must be reviewed and revised periodically as factual information and a new appraisal of political and economic trends dictate."

What, really, is the manager saying? He is saying that growth funds do not grow automatically or inevitably. They follow the general rises and falls in the stock market. The investor *must* be prepared for periods of decline in asset value.

There is something else the manager would like to say but the law forbids him to say it, that is, if the investor is truly interested in growth, then *realism* and *patience* will pay off if the past 10, 15 and 20-year periods of mutual fund history are any criteria. In Chapter

6 the historical performance of growth funds is discussed in more detail.

How Would Your Capital Grow at Compound Interest?

If you are like many people, you find compound interest figures somewhat mysterious. In trying to make a decision about investing in a mutual fund, and after studying the record of particular funds that interest you, it would be helpful for you to know the approximate growth of $1,000 if you were to keep it in a bank savings account, a savings and loan account, or a bond with a fixed yield rate.

Use the following table of the growth of $1,000 compounded at various interest rates over various periods of time. The figures have been rounded to the nearest whole dollar. When you use this table for purposes of comparisons with the capital growth of specific funds, remember that mutual fund shares fluctuate in value. Dividends vary, while the principal in a savings account or a bond is relatively stable.

Make the necessary adjustment according to your capital sum: for $100 divide all the figures by ten; for $500 divide all figures in half; for $2,000 double all figures, etc. Using the table you can determine the rate of compounding of mutual fund's growth.

Suppose that you are studying the record of a growth fund in which an assumed lump-sum investment of $1,000 would have been worth $3,000 in ten years. First, go to the 10-year column. The figure $2,960 is closest to $3,000. The figure $2,960 is what $1,000 would have become in ten years at *11%* compounded quarterly.

Follow the same procedure for the growth of a $10,000 investment, simply multiplying the figures in the columns by 10. For example, suppose a lump-sum investment of $10,000 had a value of $40,000 after ten years in a growth fund. In the 10-year column,

RATE OF CAPITAL GROWTH OF $1,000 AT COMPOUND INTEREST

Compounded Quarterly

Annual Rate %	10 Years	15 Years	20 Years	25 Years
2	$1,221	$1,349	$1,490	$1,647
2½	1,283	1,453	1,646	1,865
3	1,348	1,566	1,818	2,111
3½	1,417	1,687	2,008	2,390
4	1,489	1,817	2,217	2,705
4½	1,564	1,957	2,447	3,061
5	1,644	2,107	2,702	3,463
5½	1,727	2,269	2,982	3,918
6	1,814	2,443	3,291	4,432
6½	1,906	2,631	3,631	5,013
7	2,001	2,832	4,006	5,669
7½	2,102	3,048	4,420	6,409
8	2,208	3,281	4,875	7,245
8½	2,319	3,531	5,377	8,189
9	2,435	3,800	5,930	9,254
9½	2,557	4,089	6,540	10,457
10	2,685	4,400	7,210	11,814
10½	2,819	4,734	7,948	13,345
11	2,960	5,092	8,761	15,072
11½	3,107	5,478	9,656	17,021
12	3,262	5,892	10,641	19,219
12½	3,424	6,336	11,725	21,697
13	3,594	6,814	12,918	24,491
13½	3,772	7,327	14,231	21,697
14	3,959	7,878	15,676	31,191
15	4,360	9,105	19,013	39,702
16	4,801	10,520	23,050	50,505
17	5,285	12,150	27,931	64,211
18	5,816	14,027	33,830	81,589
19	6,400	16,190	40,957	103,610
20	7,040	18,679	49,561	131,501

(Source: Final Compound Interest and Annuity Tables, adopted from *Fund-Scope*)

find the figure which, multiplied by 10, is closest to $40,000. It is $3,959. Multiplied by ten, you have $39,590, indicating a *14%* compounding factor.

Using the table, at approximately what rate did each of the following lump-sum investments compound in a growth fund?

a) $10,000 grew to $22,000 in ten years.
b) $10,000 grew to $53,000 in ten years.
c) $10,000 grew to $91,000 in fifteen years.
d) $10,000 grew to $155,000 in twenty years.
(Answers: a) 8%   b) 17%   c) 15%   d) 14%)

Income

Not everyone can afford a sizeable investment that will yield an income on which he can live; consequently, there are few funds whose goal is income alone. Some funds seek income and growth about equally, still others seek growth with income in some ratio favoring growth. Income as the purpose of a fund, then, is a matter of degree. Conversely, some income funds also seek stability of asset value in addition to income.

Here is a quote from the prospectus of a well-known income fund:

"The _____ Fund is designed for you who are interested in current cash distributions. The primary objectives are to produce a satisfactory rate of return and to conserve the value of your investment. The management and the investment manager always keep in mind that it is the buying power of your dollars that they are endeavoring to conserve and increase, as well as the dollars themselves."

In an income fund, then, the major goal is usually *not* to increase the net asset value of a share but to secure a good yield on the investment.

Computing "Yield/Income"

We come now to a subject which often confuses new mutual fund investors and even some veterans. Like most people, you would probably consider money in your pocket from an investment as "yield." For example, if a share costs you $5.00 and the dividend is $.10 and the capital gain distribution is $.40, you would call the total of $.50 a yield of 10%.

Not so, says the Securities and Exchange Commission. Its "Statement of Policy" forbids the lumping together of dividends from investment income and capital gains distributions in calculating "yield/income." This is because capital gains distributions are considered a *return of your capital* that reduces the cost of your shares. According to the SEC, capital gains distributions are *not* income and it is a violation of SEC regulations for a fund to include capital gains distributions when computing yield on an investment.

"But," you may reply, "what's in a name? What's the difference? After all, what I want is dollars in my pocket and I don't care whether they are called 'dividends,' 'capital gains distributions,' or whatever." You are right, of course, but it is very important that you recognize the distinction for two reasons.

First, whenever you see a "Yield/Income" figure of a fund in a prospectus or chart that rates funds, remember that it includes only *dividends per share*. For example, a 2.6% "yield" means that the dividend per share paid by the fund was 2.6% of the net asset value of a share at the beginning of the period for which the dividend is being declared. *But if you want to know the yield in money in your pocket or in new shares acquired by reinvestment of distributions, then be sure to add the dividends and the capital gains distributions to figure the return.*

For example, a share costing $10.00 at the beginning of the year which paid a dividend of $.10 will be *legally* described as having a yield/income of 1%. Now, suppose the capital gains distribution per share was $1.00. Add that to the dividend of $.10 and you have $1.10 per share in the pocket or in reinvested distributions to buy additional shares. On an investment of $10.00 a share, $1.10 is a return of 11%.

To repeat: for *your* own purposes in calculating what a fund's rate of return would have been for you, either in your pocket or in reinvestments for more shares in your account, start with the net asset value of a share at the beginning of a dividend period. Then add together the dividend and the capital gains distributions per share. Divide the beginning-of-the-year net asset value per share into the sum of the dividend and capital gains distributions and you can calculate the return on your investment.

Study the following figures from the 1967 performance of an actual fund and then see whether you can answer the questions that follow them.

1. Net asset value of a share at the beginning of
the year $12.00
2. Net asset value of a share at the end of the
year   13.50
3. Income dividends per share paid during the
year   .20
4. Capital gains distributions per share paid during the year   1.00

QUESTIONS

1. What was the yield/income as the SEC would require it to be stated in the fund's brochure, by a broker, an official of the fund management, or in statistical analysis of the fund's performance?

2. What was the "in the pocket" or "reinvestment" return per share?

3. What is the percentage of total growth in a share's value for the year?
(Answers: 1) 1⅔%   2) 10%   3) 12½%)

The second reason why you must distinguish between yield/income and capital gains distributions is for income tax purposes. Capital gains distributions, like yield/income from dividends, are reportable for income tax but *how* they are taxed depends on whether they were *short-term* (received in the pocket within six months or less) or *long-term* (received in the pocket or in reinvestment in shares after six months or more).

Now you know why there are growth funds which seek income secondarily but which will actually provide more gross income (dividends plus capital gains distributions) than a so-called "income only" fund. The only way to discover such a fund is by studying fund performances for yourself or to ask a broker for help in locating one (Chapter 15).

A return on an investment is either an actual or a potential return whether it is in dividends, capital gains distributions, an increase in the net asset value of a share, or all of these combined. When you begin calculating past or present returns on an investment in a mutual fund, remember to consider all these figures.

Stability

Stability means "capital preservation." Your capital may be well-preserved in a fund when there is no excessive fluctuation in the price of the share. The best standard to use in assessing a fund's stability is to examine carefully the history of its performance in declining market periods. You would hardly complain about instability that was always upward!

When you scan market periods of the past to gauge a fund's

stability, do not assume that the fund will necessarily repeat its performance. The past is only a map showing when management was right and when it was wrong in relation to its stated investment objective. The past is not necessarily an indicator of future performance; however, if a management group has been successful in achieving its management objective consistently in the past, it is more likely that it has the potential to do so again.

It is very important to remember that certain types of funds have a "built-in protection" against instability in declining markets. That cushion is a substantial amount of bonds and preferred stocks in the fund's portfolio. Many "income only" funds fall into this category. While the net asset value of a share in an income fund does not usually increase substantially, neither does it usually drop substantially. The investor wants stable capital that yields regular income dividends.

The biggest mistake that a "stability-seeker" can make is to expect it from a fund whose primary purpose is growth. A growth fund will ordinarily be willing to take a greater degree of risk with capital than will an income fund. Volatile stocks and constant trading of portfolio holdings can make a fund's per share value fluctuate. A second common mistake made by stability seekers in a fund is to assume that any drop in its net asset value per share is a black mark against it. What one should look for is the percentage of decline as compared with that of other mutual funds of a similar type.

Four market decline periods that may be helpfully used for examination of a fund's price stability are (1) July through October, 1957, (2) January through September, 1960, (3) January through June, 1962 and (4) February through September, 1966.

There are two methods commonly used to rank price stability in a fund. First, in declining markets, compare the fund's stability with other funds having similar investment objectives. One well-known growth fund's asset value decreased 8% in 1962 while another growth fund lost 16% in asset value in the same period. Another growth fund dropped 14% in asset value in 1966 compared with the 5% average decrease in asset value of all growth funds. In addition to the rate of decline in a falling market, you should also compare the rates of recovery among funds with similar investment objectives. As was previously stated, one fund's asset value declined 16% in 1962 compared with another growth fund that declined only 8%; however, the first fund's asset value rose 31% in 1967, while the second fund's rose only 10%.

Establishing a Fund's Stability by Comparing It with Stock List Averages

The second common method of establishing a fund's stability is to compare its increase or decrease in asset value per share with the average price fluctuations of some well-known list of stocks, like the Dow Jones Industrial Average of 30 common stocks or Standard & Poor's 500 Stock Average or the New York Stock Exchange Composite Index. Most rankings and ratings of fund performance consider the stock averages the most suggestive indicator of trends in the economy as reflected in the buying and selling of securities. The comparisons are not only convenient but also often dramatic. They are comfortable and conventional, having been dignified by habit and custom. Since the stock market consists of innumerable variables, establishing stock averages for purposes of comparison brings some order out of an infinite variety of causal relationships.

Some mutual funds have established a sliding management fee that goes up if the fund beats the Dow Jones averages by some mathematical percentage. Promising new funds are often identified by their superior performance over the averages; older, well-established funds use the comparisons prominently in assessing long-term performance of their funds.

A Note of Caution

Sometimes the signposts of the most popular stock lists contradict each other because those lists represent different samplings of different types of stock. One should be cautious about drawing definitive conclusions when he compares a mutual fund's performance with the "average" performance of a list of stocks because much may depend on the stock list used. Consider, for example, this story from the Associated Press of July 15, 1968.

"WHICH STOCK INDEX CAN YOU BELIEVE?

"New York (AP)—Two big, broad signposts of the stock market have been telling investors the market has been making historic highs this year (1968), but not the Dow Jones Industrial Average.

"The Dow Industrials, most closely watched signpost of them all, shows the market last reached an all-time closing high of 995.15 on February 9, 1966, and has not come close to it since.

"On the other hand, the broad-gauged indexes of Standard & Poor's Corp. and the New York Stock Exchange say the market has made record peaks repeatedly this year.

"Why the different stories?

"In a nutshell, the laggard showing of the Dow average is due to the fact it is composed of 30 of the biggest and best blue chips. These stocks have fallen behind the newer and more exciting growth stocks in market performances—and they are amply represented in the S&P and the New York Exchange indexes.

"Another factor is that the Dow Industrials represent only 30 stocks, while Standard & Poor's has an index of 500 stocks and the New York Exchange index is of all 1,250 common stocks listed on the Big Board.

"Where does the investor really get the answer to his question, 'How's the market'?

"The serious student of the market may find Standard & Poor's offers a scientific approach. Aside from its 500 stock index—which is broken up into 425 industrials, 20 railroads and 55 utilities—S&P offers every week 89 other indexes of stocks representing separate industries and businesses.

"It has been said many times on Wall Street:

"It's a market of stocks rather than a stock market!"

If the signposts of the most popular stock lists may contradict each other because those lists represent different samplings of different types of stocks, one should be aware of this when he compares a mutual fund's performance with the "average" performance of a list of stocks. Perhaps, with computers being used increasingly in stock market transactions, we may hopefully see the day when *every* stock traded on the New York Stock Exchange and American Exchange will be considered in compiling a net market trend, i.e., each individual stock's advance would be offset by a similar decline in another individual stock's price so that *on balance* it could be determined daily in which direction the market is moving.

5   Who Rates the Funds and How?

"What mutual fund will do the best job for me?" is the first question that you, and thousands like you, ask. With over 300 funds in existence, and another 100 or so on the near horizon, how can you make a choice? Help is available.

A. *FundScope.*   *FundScope* is a monthly magazine prepared for mutual fund investors. It is totally committed to the premise that mutual funds are an outstanding type of long-term investment. It will defend mutual funds when they are the object of what it considers unfair criticism as it did in an article titled, "FundScope Exposes 'True' Magazine," in August, 1964, replying to an article in *True,* ("The Money-Making Myth of Mutual Funds") published in July, 1964.

The stated editorial policy of *FundScope* is as follows:

"We try for painstaking accuracy so that *FundScope* will be accepted universally without question as the outstanding independent authority in the field. We emphasize 'independent' because unlike some other publications, *FundScope* does not publish a stock market advisory service, we do not manage or solicit investment accounts,

---

* Material from *Forbes, FundScope,* and Arthur Wiesenberger Services Division of Nuveen Corporation, by permission.

we are not brokers or dealers, we do not belong to any stock exchange or mutual fund trade association, we do not sell mutual fund shares, we do not recommend individual funds, we have no connection of any kind whatsoever with any mutual fund or any mutual fund management company or any mutual fund distributor.

"In short, edited from the investor's viewpoint, *FundScope* has no axe to grind and we carry no torch for individual funds. *FundScope* is a magazine of fact, not opinions, and lets the record speak for itself."

Each December *FundScope* rates all funds for their past 10-year performance and their annual performance, providing a detailed explanation of how the ratings are determined. It rates funds as "above average" or "below average" for three qualities: growth, income, and stability. A fund is not rated if its history is too brief to furnish a guide, if there is a question as to whether or not it qualifies for an above average or below average rating, or if essential data is missing. A sample reproduction of one of *Fund-Scope's* rating methods looks like this:

GROUP [1]	GROWTH RATING	INCOME RATING	STABILITY RATING
Fund 1 1-dcs	*	—	—
Fund 2 3-fd	*	*	*
Fund 3 1-sd	—	—	—
* Above average			
— Below average			

[1] For fund classifications, see Chapter 15.

In the same December issue, in a separate alphabetical ranking of the 10-year results and the yearly results, *FundScope* also indicates the top 25 funds (a) in cash dividends yielded, with capital gains distributions reinvested; (b) in liquidating value (dividends and capital gains distributions reinvested). Here is a sample cut of those ratings.

The results shown is a record of the past. Under no circumstances should this data be construed as a forecast of the future dividend income or capital gain or loss which may be realized from an investment made in the funds today.

In all tabulations in this issue of *FundScope*, investors should consider any fund mentioned in the light of its currently effective prospectus.

(*) *Performed Better Than Average For Period Indicated*

(**) *In "Top 25," or "Top 10%" For Period Indicated*

MUTUAL FUND GUIDE—SUPPLEMENT

In This Tabulation, Funds Are Listed By Group Classification

Group	GROWTH-APPRECIATION RECORD *Rising Market Periods*						INCOME RECORD *Yield/Dividends*			STABILITY RECORD	
	% A.V. Gain or Loss 1963	% A.V. Gain or Loss 1964	% A.V. Gain or Loss 1965	Twelve Months 9/30/66 to 9/30/67	5-Year Liquid. Value (2) Average Past 5 5-Year Periods	10-Year Liquid. Value (2) Average Past 5 10-Year Periods	% Yield 9/30 1967	5-Year Total Cash Dividends (1)	10-Year Total Cash Dividends (1)	% A.V. Gain or Loss 12/31/61 to 6/28/62	% A.V. Gain or Loss 2/9/66 to 10/7/66
Fund #1	+10.3	+4.2	+23.6*	+42.2*	NA	NA	1.14	NA	NA	−30.7	−18.0*
Fund #2	X	X	X	+43.7	X	X	1.33	X	X	X	X
Fund #3	+6.9	+4.1	+16.8	+60.0*	11,480	X	1.17	689	2,017	−33.2	−19.9
Fund #4	+15.6	+11.7	+25.3*	+41.6*	14,899*	32,956**	1.59	883	2,352	−24.6	−12.0**
Fund #5	+16.6*	+12.1	+38.7**	+47.9*	12,763	29,770*	0.79	433	1,486	−38.8	−22.3
Fund #6	+21.5*	+22.3**	+47.6**	+57.2*	X	X	0.61	669	X	X	−25.8
Fund #7	+24.7**	+16.4*	+28.7**	+38.2**	17,526**	45,704**	1.64	1,020	3,777*	−24.5	−19.7
Fund #8	X	X	+6.8	+36.9	X	X	1.65	X	X	X	−18.4*
Fund #9	+21.3*	+9.0	+28.4*	+53.8*	15,980*	X	1.30	761	2,048	−29.6	−19.9
Fund #10	+28.0**	+24.0**	+40.2**	+119.0**	NA	NA	0.27	NA	NA	−27.7	−28.4

Source for Data

Asset Value, Gain or Loss for individual years 1962 through 1966, taken from April 1967 Mutual Fund Guide. Except period 12/31/1962 to 6/28/62, taken from March 1963 FundScope; and period 2/9/66 to 10/7/66 taken from January 1967 FundScope; and period 9/30/66 to 9/30/67 taken from November 1967 FundScope.

Current Yield as of September 30, 1967 taken from November 1967 FundScope.

5-Year Dividends from May 1967 FundScope. 10-Year Dividends from April 1967 Mutual Fund Guide. 5-Year Average

Liquidating Value from October 1967 FundScope. 10-Year Average Liquidating Value from July 1967 FundScope.

(1) Total of dividends from investment income paid in cash, based on initial $10,000 investment with capital gains distributions reinvested in stock, period ending 12/31/1966.

(2) Based on initial $10,000 investment, represents average Liquidating Value (past five periods) assuming all distributions reinvested in stock.

(A.V.) Asset Value. Gain or loss adjusted for all distributions (dividends and capital gains.)

(X) Not applicable; or in existence less than period indicated.

(NA) Not Available.

FundScope's rankings and ratings of funds enable you to compare funds with similar investment objectives. It is an excellent publication in its scope, depth and detail of data. Its monthly coverage of fund facts is comprehensive and it provides helpful articles on all facets of fund investing.

B. *Forbes* magazine pointed up the investor's problem in its August 15, 1966, issue when it wrote:

> "When the editors of *Forbes* produced their first annual report on mutual funds back in the summer of 1956, we knew we were filling a need . . . there was no handy way for the investor to get a fast, impartial answer to an important question: 'What mutual fund would do the best job for me?'
>
> "True, there were the figures published by the funds themselves. But these were numbers in a vacuum. They didn't show how the individual fund stacked up against other funds. There was also at least one other publication that reported comparative figures on a quarterly basis, but it was—and still is—*Forbes'* firm conviction that such short-term measurements are meaningless. When an investor pays 8% or more in commissions, he isn't investing for just three or six months.
>
> "Ever since the first survey appeared in 1956, *Forbes'* statisticians have been working hard to improve our methods of measurement. Today we think that they are about as fair, meaningful and impartial as we can make them. The important thing is this: these are not merely raw numbers; they are an attempt to render a qualitative judgment on mutual fund performance from the numbers themselves."

Each August *Forbes* rates the funds. Its emphasis is on a speedy, impartial answer for the investor, based on careful, statistical analysis. What, exactly, does *Forbes* rate? It rates *consistency of performance*. The ratings are based on the premise that a fund's performance can be best evaluated by comparing it with the performance of lists of stocks.

Applying a carefully worked-out set of standards to fund performance, *Forbes'* statisticians grade the funds on a scale ranging from A plus to D minus. They rate funds on the basis of performance in four rising markets and four declining markets. The four periods of rising markets are (1) October, 1957, through December, 1959; (2) October, 1960, through December, 1961; (3) July, 1962, through January, 1966; (4) October, 1966, through April, 1967. The four periods of declining markets are (1) July through September, 1957; (2) January through September, 1960; (3) January through June, 1962; (4) February through September, 1966.

For each "up" period, *Forbes'* researchers ask, "Did the fund do better than the (Standard & Poor) average? Did it merely keep up? Or did it actually fall behind the averages?" Funds that managed to keep up with Standard & Poor's 500 Stock Average in all four of the rising market periods receive a B plus for consistency. Funds that keep up three times get a B; twice, a C plus; once, a C. Funds that do poorer than the averages in all four periods receive an F. A fund that succeeded not only in outperforming the average every time but in outperforming it by 20% or better rates an A plus; by 10% to 19.9% an A. A fund that was consistently beaten by the averages by a margin of 10% rates a D minus. A similar rating system is applied to "down" periods. No ratings are given when a fund did not exist for at least two up and two down periods.

In addition to rating fund consistency of performance, *Forbes* also reports management results by telling you how $100 of your money would have ended up (a) at the end of the most recent five years; (b) at the end of the latest twelve months; (c) in terms of % dividend return. It hastens to add:

"A fund may look better in sheer dollar figures than it does in the Consistency Ratings—or vice versa. Reason: Dollar figures are more easily distorted by one dramatic good or poor period."

Any ratings of funds, or any reports of fund performance, must either ignore load (sales) charges or include them in performance results. None of the loading charges (from 8.5% to 1%) is taken into account by the *Forbes'* ratings. As they put it

". . . the ratings are intended to measure management skill in handling money rather than the actual investment results."

Forbes then goes on to tell you in simple terms how to determine how much the loading charge affects dollar performance. The magazine does not measure the balanced funds against the Standard & Poor Index. Instead, it measures them against the average performance of the 10 largest balanced funds in its survey (however, size is not necessarily a criterion of performance).

Rounding out its rating tables, *Forbes* also gives the assets of each fund, the maximum sales charge and the annual expense of the fund in cents per $100. Study the sample cut from the August, 1968, issue of *Forbes* to get the feel of its rating system.

C. *Annual and Quarterly Reports of Management Results in Investment Companies* published by Arthur Wiesenberger Services Division of Nuveen Corporation. This is a well-known, technical publication. It is highlighted here for three reasons: first, a broker who tries to sell you an investment in a fund probably uses it as a source of information and a basis for evaluating a fund; second, it is noted for its thoroughness and objectivity; third, it is the only publication of its kind.

The "management results" are not "ratings" in the ordinary sense but, rather, reference statistics which are supplementary to the extensive fund descriptions contained in the annual textbook and manual, *Investment Companies*. The latter, published each year since 1941, is a widely known publication generally available at brokerage offices and many public libraries.

Sample Cut of Forbes' Rating Scale of Mutual Funds

Assets in Millions	Maximum Sales Charge %	Annual Expenses (Cents per $100)	FUND RATINGS	CONSISTENCY OF PERFORMANCE		MANAGEMENT RESULTS		Div. Return %
				In UP Markets	In DOWN Markets	$100 Ended As 1962–1967	Last 12 Months	
			Standard & Poor's			165.55	106.96	3.2
			Average of 10 stock funds in *Forbes* Index	B	C plus	186.54	109.95	2.4
			STOCK FUNDS (Load)					
$ 44.5	8.50	$0.81	Fund A	B	C	183.75	107.96	1.6
$374.9	8.50	0.61	Fund B	B	B	179.86	111.90	2.7
			STOCK FUNDS (No Load)					
79.6	None	0.81	Fund C	B plus	C plus	230.06	127.91	1.3

The annual volume covers the preceding ten years and shows, for virtually every mutual fund with assets of $5 million or more and at least one calendar year of operation, management results for individual years and for periods of varying length. Quarterly supplements, made available to purchasers of the annual book, show the latest interim period, the previous years, and the preceding five-and-a-fraction and ten-and-a-fraction years. The funds are grouped in various categories, depending upon the funds' objectives and policies; within these groups, the arrangement is alphabetical.

In *Investment Companies 1968* the following explanation is given:

> "Performance statistics are intended only to provide a convenient measure of relative management capabilities in relation to stated objectives, to the extent that they can be measured by past results. For this purpose, the data are limited to what management has accomplished with the money at its disposal, divorced from various factors over which management has little or no control. The latter include such things as varying sales charges, in the case of mutual funds; changing discounts or premiums, or the effects of senior capital, in the case of closed-end companies; taxes payable by the investor and the choice he may make in regard to reinvesting either capital gains distributions or income dividends.
>
> "Thus, the data are not intended to be, and are not, a record of shareholder experience. They are a rough measure of caliber of management, against which the investor can weigh the relative importance of differences in sales charges, in discounts or premiums, and in various other considerations that may influence the choice of a particular fund."

Study the sample reproduction from the March, 1968, issue of the Wiesenberger report to see the kind of data it makes available.

D. *Additional Sources of Rankings.* There are other annual, semiannual and monthly publications whose fund rankings may help you evaluate fund performance. One of the most popular is

SAMPLE CUT FROM WIESENBERGER'S INVESTMENT COMPANIES

APPROXIMATE PERCENT CHANGE IN NET ASSETS PER SHARE WITH CAPITAL GAINS (REINVESTED) PLUS INCOME DIVIDENDS (RECEIVED IN CASH)

	Total Net Assets 3/1/68	3 Months 1968	Year 1967	5½ Years 1963 to 3/1/68	10½ Years 1958 to 3/1/68	Classification of Assets March 31, 1968			
						Cash & Govts.	Bonds & Pfds.	Common Stocks	Return
I. GROWTH FUNDS									
A. LARGE (1967 Year-End Assets Over $300,000,000)									
Fund A	284.8	−15.8	46.7	131.3	207.0	13%	4%	83%	0.8%
B. SMALLER (Objective: Maximum Capital Gain. Volatility: Generally High)									
Fund B	44.0	−17.4	67.8	150.1	295.8	25%	15%	60%	0.2%
II. OTHER DIVERSIFIED COMMON STOCK FUNDS									
A. OBJECTIVE GROWTH AND CURRENT INCOME (Volatility: Average)									
Fund C	133.3	−5.5	22.7	71.0	166.8	13%	—	87%	2.7%
B. OBJECTIVE: GROWTH AND CURRENT INCOME, WITH RELATIVE STABILITY (Volatility: Below Average)									
Fund D	36.8	−4.2	38.0	92.2	198.8	32%	2%	66%	1.9%
III. BALANCED FUNDS									
Fund E	69.2	−11.0	58.1	123.8	214.9	8%	29%	63%	1.6%
IV. INCOME FUNDS									
Fund F	50.4	0.2	16.7	72.0	161.6	14%	28%	58%	3.8%
V. SPECIALIZED FUNDS									
A. INSURANCE AND BANK STOCKS									
Fund G	63.8	−7.0	3.1	−17.5	98.1	2%	—	98%	2.0%
B. CANADIAN AND INTERNATIONAL ISSUES......									
C. PUBLIC UTILITY STOCKS......									
D. CONVERTIBLE BONDS AND PREFERRED STOCKS									
**VI. TAX-FREE EXCHANGE FUNDS......									

the Johnson Company's *Investment Company Charts,* which has special charts and overlays for performance analysis. Other publications, which may or may not clear their material with the SEC, report on and analyze short-term mutual fund performance, rating the funds in some fashion from A to C or from "Excellent" to "Below Average." Also provided are the names and addresses of funds which are rated, to which the reader is urged to write for prospectuses, and the reminder that past performance is no guarantee of future performance. Some of these publications advertise; others do not. See Appendix I for more sources of information.

If you wish to inquire about the reputability of any publication that ranks and rates funds in any way, it is suggested that you write to Mr. James Ratzlaff, Director, Investment Companies Department, National Association of Securities Dealers, Inc., 888 Seventeenth Street, N.W., Washington, D.C.

6   The Record of Performance

In the last analysis only one thing counts with an investment: performance which meets your investment objectives. Say what they will, the detractors of mutual funds cannot ignore or deny what the funds have done. To my knowledge, the staunchest fund advocate makes no sweeping claims about the inherent superiority of mutual funds, he does not disparage investing in individual stocks, and he does not insist that a mutual fund will *necessarily* outperform other kinds of stock investments. He does assert that many mutual funds are an excellent long-term investment. He may also state that superior funds could perform extraordinarily well, and that funds in general offer the average citizen a variety of appealing elements which are congenial to his pocketbook, his psychology and his expectations for the future.

When one inquires about the "performance" of an investment, he wants the answers to three questions: performance in what? performance in comparison with what? and performance over what period of time?

Growth Comparisons Among Funds Over 5, 10, 15, and 20-Year Periods*

Let us now look at the growth performance of funds among themselves (that is, compared with each other). And let us consider 5, 10, 15 and 20-year periods because the funds are long-term investments. The number of funds being compared will vary somewhat among and within the periods because new ones have been coming into existence every year in the last quarter century.

FIVE-YEAR GROWTH OF A $10,000 LUMP-SUM INVESTMENT

In the past 21 years there have been seventeen 5-year periods.

Results for individual funds ranged from a liquidating value of $47,409 for the top fund down to $7,248 for a Bond Fund.

In the best period, the average liquidation value was $21,376, or more than *double* the original investment.

One fund had a liquidating value greater than $45,000, 7 funds had more than $35,000, 15 funds had more than $30,000 and 32 funds had more than $25,000.

The latest 5-year period was among the best in the past 21 years whereas the preceding 5-year period ending in 1966 was the worst, due to the stock market declines of 1962 and 1966.

Remember! Fund values go *down* as well as up! Be prepared.

Figures assume reinvestment of all divi-

In the table below are ranked, *in descending order,* average results for each of the seventeen 5-year periods.

AVERAGE MUTUAL FUND RESULTS OF A $10,000 INVESTMENT

Five-Year Period	Liquidating Value
1954–1958	$21,376
1950–1954	21,330
1951–1955	20,572
1963–1967	19,397
1952–1956	19,168
1959–1963	17,089
1948–1952	17,062
1958–1962	17,018
1957–1961	16,383
1955–1959	16,338
1961–1965	16,268
1953–1957	15,406
1947–1951	15,120
1956–1960	14,399
1960–1964	14,326
1959–1963	14,295
1962–1966	12,429

* Data from *FundScope* by permission. 1968 data was not available at the time of writing.

dends and capital gains distributions. They are established after deducting all costs.

(Liquidating Value: Results of a $10,000 lump-sum investment with all distributions reinvested. No adjustment made for income taxes. For a $5,000 investment, divide by 2. For a $1,000 investment, divide by 10.)

(Data from *FundScope,* May, 1968, p. 23.)

TEN-YEAR GROWTH OF A $10,000 LUMP-SUM INVESTMENT

Within the past quarter century (since January 1, 1943), there have been sixteen 10-year periods.

Assuming a hypothetical initial investment of $10,000 at the start of each period, no fund at the end of *any* 10-year period would have been liquidated for less than $10,000.

Taking a composite average of the 10-year table, the worst of all 10-year periods was 1957–1966, when the average cash-in value at the end was $21,735, or over *double* the original investment.

The average cash-in value for *all* funds in all the 10-year periods in the last quarter century was $29,336, or nearly *triple* the original investment.

The best of all 10-year periods was 1949–1958, when average cash-in value for all funds was $39,087.

The results for individual funds ranged from a low of $10,835 to a high of $210,-559 in the various 10-year periods, reflecting the great variation in results among mutual funds.

Figures assume reinvestment of all divi-

In the table below are ranked, *in descending order,* average results for each of the sixteen 10-year periods.

AVERAGE MUTUAL FUND RESULTS OF A $10,000 INVESTMENT

Five-Year Period	Liquidating Value
1949–1958	$39,087
1950–1959	37,170
1943–1952	33,637
1952–1961	33,203
1958–1967	33,184
1951–1960	31,321
1954–1963	31,230
1947–1956	31,081
1945–1954	30,354
1948–1957	27,724
1953–1962	26,838
1946–1955	26,650
1944–1953	26,019
1956–1965	24,499
1955–1964	24,367
1957–1966	21,735

(Liquidating Value: Results of a $10,000 lump-sum investment with all distributions reinvested. No adjustment made for income taxes. For a $5,000 investment,

dends and capital gains distributions. They are established after deducting *all* costs, commissions and fees.

FIFTEEN-YEAR GROWTH OF A $10,000 LUMP-SUM INVESTMENT

Within the past quarter century there were eleven 15-year periods. No fund in any 15-year period would have been liquidated for less than $10,000.

Average results for *all* funds in *all* 11 periods was $51,899.

In the worst period of all 11, a $10,000 investment on January 1, 1946, showed an average liquidation value of $40,160 on December 31, 1960.

In the worst period individual fund results varied greatly from the average; they ranged from a low of $12,775 to a high of $70,895.

In the best of all 15-year periods, 1944–1958, the average liquidation value for all funds on a $10,000 lump-sum investment at the end of the period was $60,372, or *six times* the original investment.

In the various 15-year periods, individual funds registered results as low as $12,585 and as high as $158,574.

Figures assume reinvestment of all dividends and capital gains distributions. They are established after deducting *all* costs.

divide by 2. For a $1,000 investment, divide by 10.)

(Data from *FundScope,* July, 1968, p. 16.)

In the table below are ranked, *in descending order,* average results for each of the eleven 15-year periods.

AVERAGE MUTUAL FUND RESULTS OF A $10,000 INVESTMENT

15-Year Period	Liquidating Value
1944–1958	$60,372
1949–1963	57,013
1943–1957	56,421
1950–1964	55,260
1951–1965	54,544
1945–1959	54,377
1947–1961	53,937
1953–1967	52,159
1948–1962	48,490
1952–1966	45,331
1946–1960	40,160

(Liquidating Value: Results of a $10,000 lump-sum investment with all distributions reinvested. No adjustment made for income taxes. For a $5,000 investment, divide by 2. For a $1,000 investment, divide by 10.)

(Data from *FundScope,* July, 1968, p. 16.)

TWENTY-YEAR GROWTH OF A $10,000 LUMP-SUM INVESTMENT

There were six 20-year periods within the past quarter century; 71 funds have been in existence 20 years or longer.

Not one of the 71 funds would have been liquidated for less than $10,000 in any 20-year period.

Average liquidation value for *all* funds in *all* 20-year periods was $83,985, or more than *eight times* the original investment.

In the *worst* of all 20-year periods, 1946–1965, average cash-in value at the end was $69,158. Individual funds ranged from a low of $12,245 for a bond fund to a high of $134,442 for an aggressive common stock fund.

In the *best* of all 20-year periods, 1943–1962, average cash-in value was $99,038. Results for individual funds ranged from a low of $19,211 for a very conservative bond fund to a high of $225,771 for an aggressive stock fund.

In various 20-year periods, individual funds showed a cash-in value as low as $12,245 and as high as $238,149.

Figures assume reinvestment of all dividends and capital gains distributions. They are established after deducting *all* costs.

In the table below are ranked, *in descending order,* average results for each of the six 20-year periods.

AVERAGE MUTUAL FUND RESULTS OF A $10,000 INVESTMENT

20-Year Period	Liquidating Value
1943–1962	$99,038
1948–1967	90,112
1944–1963	88,761
1945–1964	80,977
1947–1966	71,961
1946–1965	69,158

(Liquidating Value: Results of a $10,000 lump-sum investment with all distributions reinvested. No adjustment made for income taxes. For a $5,000 investment, divide by 2. For a $1,000 investment, divide by 10.)

(Data from *FundScope,* July, 1968, p. 16.)

*Growth Performance Among Funds in a Recent One-Year Period.**

Assessing a year's growth performance of a mutual fund is like trying to appraise the yield of planted corn after a month. The fund's growth, like the corn stalk, might be promising or it might look emaciated. Just as the corn needs to germinate and is dependent upon the husbandry of the grower, the changing weather, the soil conditions, and the quality of the seedling, so does the fund's growth depend on management, changing market conditions, and the developments in national and international affairs.

From March 31, 1967, to March 31, 1968, one fund gained as much as 127.3% in asset value and one fund lost as much as 15.5% in asset value; two funds gained more than 90%, six funds gained more than 40%, ten funds gained more than 30%, and seventeen funds gained more than 25%. Of 255 funds, 207 had a gain for these twelve months and 48 had a loss in asset value. The average gain for all mutual funds for this 12-month period was 8.2%.

The biggest mistake a mutual fund investor can make is to assess a fund's performance in terms of a brief period like 3 months, 6 months, or a year; yet, some investors and brokers like to draw immediate conclusions about the worthiness of an investment. To them, the most compelling evidence seems to be the most recent evidence even though it is the most misleading and the most inconclusive.

Conclusions from the Growth Data Among Mutual Funds

What does the preceding data mean to a mutual fund investor who seeks growth in his capital investment? First, no single period of any length in the last quarter century is typical of mutual fund

* *FundScope,* May, 1968.

performance. Second, there is no way to tell which period will prove to be the best, or the worst, over a number of years. It is the price level at the start and at the end of a given period that determines the end results, and the ending price level cannot be foreseen. Third, though some periods will probably be much better than others, any period seems to be a good time to invest in mutual funds for the long-term.

Fourth, to be sure that some purchases will be made at important market bottoms, and not only at market tops, at least part of your total mutual fund investments should be spread systematically over a period of years long enough to include one or more major market declines. This is known as "dollar-cost averaging" and is discussed on page 35. Again, the longer you hold your shares, the greater are the odds in your favor for good capital appreciation, especially if you reinvest all capital gains and dividends. Fifth, careful, systematic selection of individual mutual funds is important if you seek average or better than average results in capital appreciation. Finally, reduce risk in selecting funds by investing in a *package* of funds rather than concentrating all your capital in one fund; in other words, diversify your fund portfolio.

It must be emphasized that all growth data shown are a record of the past. They must not be construed as a prediction of future growth.

Income Performance

What do you want from an investment: a current income which is relatively high while your capital is being preserved, or a current income which is relatively low with an opportunity for growth of capital? This question requires you to think about a very important difference between two purposes of a mutual fund: *current income* or *growth of capital*.

If you want income, the performance of income funds will interest you the most. These invest in common and preferred stocks or bonds whose income yield is consistent and relatively high. If you seek growth, growth funds will probably appeal to you most because they invest in securities with the objective of achieving capital gains.

The income from a growth-income (balanced) fund may or may not be much larger in the future than the income received from an income fund. Because of favorable market conditions for the past ten years, a number of growth-income funds now provide a better income yield than income funds. The distinction between current income and the potential for growth of income is not apparent in the income performance figures of funds. It tends to become obscured and blurred by the differences between the averages of all funds and the yield of the income funds alone.

Income Performance Among Funds in a Recent One-Year Period.*

Like the growth performance of a mutual fund, the income performance cannot be conclusively assessed on the basis of only a year. Many funds reveal a consistency of performance over long periods. Short-term results for funds may vary from year to year as they are influenced by temporary changes in business and stock market trends.

The average yield of 255 mutual funds for the period from March 31, 1967, to March 31, 1968, was 1.78%, or a little over 1¾ cents on the dollar. This was down slightly from the 1.99% in the previous period and the 1.91% of two years earlier. Seven bond and preferred stock funds led the field with an average of 4.70%, while fifteen income funds had an average of 4.12%. As usual, a large number of growth funds (143) had a low 0.76% average, thus pulling down the 255 fund average.

* *FundScope,* May, 1968.

The 1967–1968 period was a hectic one, marked by ups and downs because of the war in Vietnam, the gold "rush," inflation, former President Johnson's decision not to seek a second term, racial disorders, and Federal surtax uncertainties.

Income Performance Among Mutual Funds for the Five-Year Period of 1963–1967 *

At the end of 1967 there were over 300 funds that were five years old. Available data from 183 of them will show you how you might have fared, on the average, had you invested in a fund on January 1, 1963.

Assuming that you invested $1,000, the average dividend for all 183 funds was $137 or about 2½ percent a year, which is below average compared to similar periods in the past. You must remember, however, that 1966 saw one of the most serious market declines in the past 10 years.

As you may have expected, growth funds had the lowest average dividends (about $87). Income funds performed best with an average dividend of $258. One fund paid $327 while another paid nothing. Nine funds exceeded $250 in dividends while twenty-nine exceeded $200. Of the best income-yielding funds, none was among the best capital appreciation funds.

Limited Data. Did you wonder why only 183 funds could be summed up for five-year income performance while there were over 300 funds in existence by the end of 1967? Many funds are very reluctant to furnish five-year data to any publication that wishes to rate their performance (although the SEC regulations require them to furnish that data in their prospectuses). Most mutual funds charge a commission when shares are bought (8½% on the average). The funds figure that this sales charge should be amortized

* *FundScope,* May, 1968.

over a period of at least ten and preferably 15 or 20 years. Naturally, the shorter the period in which the sales charge has to be "written off," the more it depresses dollar results.

Income Performance Among Mutual Funds for the Ten-Year Period of 1958–1967 *

By the close of 1967 there were about 150 mutual funds that were ten or more years old. What kind of income dividends would you have received had you invested in one of them on January 1, 1958? Remember, income dividends are the cash amount that you would have received while having your capital gains distributions reinvested in additional shares.

Assuming that you invested $1,000, the average dividend yield for these 150 funds in the 10-year period was $382.50 or 3.8¼% annually. Keep in mind that this was only the *cash* dividend and does not include capital gains distributions, both of which should be considered in measuring your *total* investment return. As a cash dividend figure, this is well above average. As an all-fund average, however, it is significantly lower than the average for specific types of funds like income funds. Growth funds and performance funds (high rises and steep declines) do *not* aim at income dividends and therefore pull down the all-fund average.

Income only funds averaged $636 in dividends over this 10-year period. Growth and income funds averaged $500 in dividends for the same period. One balanced stock fund averaged $453 in dividends, and one bond and preferred stock fund averaged $506. One individual fund paid dividends as high as $731 and another paid none. Thirteen funds paid dividends of more than $600 and twenty-four funds paid dividends of more than $500.

Had you been able to afford an investment of $2,000, $3,000, $4,000, or $5,000, multiply all the above dividend figures by 2, 3,

* *FundScope,* April, 1968.

4, or 5, respectively. In studying the prospectuses of the fund(s) that you are considering as an investment, you may wish to use the above figures as a reference.

Conclusions About Income Performance in Mutual Funds

It is extremely difficult to combine in one mutual fund maximum growth and maximum yield income. You must weigh one alternative more heavily than the other when you choose your funds. Remember that growth funds and performance funds produce the least current income. Income funds tend to cluster around a 6% return which may be considered adequate if you are in a monthly withdrawal plan where you don't want your principal diminished.

Any mutual fund yielding dividends above 1.78% in 1967–1968 could be called "above average" in that category for that period. Income performance figures do not indicate substantial differences between *current income* funds and *growth-income* (balanced) funds. It is essential to assess a fund's income performance in terms of the fund's stated investment policy as well as in terms of the income figure alone.

Stability Performance

Between 1930 and 1940 the American economy was in serious trouble. In that decade 600 closed-end investment companies failed; 12,837 commercial banks closed their doors; 1,606 savings and loan associations went bankrupt. Approximately 14% of all life insurance companies were in reorganization or receivership. However, none of the mutual funds in existence failed. Throughout the thirties most mutual funds regularly paid dividends though in smaller amounts. Furthermore, no diversified common stock mutual fund has ever gone bankrupt or become insolvent. An investor concerned about the stability of mutual funds should consider this record.

As explained in Chapter 4, stability in a mutual fund is the degree of resistance to loss in net asset value per share in declining markets. Two decline periods for assessing such stability among funds are January 1, 1962 to June 28, 1962, and February 9, 1966 to October 7, 1966. In the first period (1962) the average decline in net asset value per share among 261 funds was 21.5% while the Dow Jones Industrial Average was down 23.7% (21.6% when adjusted for dividends paid). In the second period (1966) the 261-fund average decline was 19.6% while the Dow Jones Industrial Average was down 25.2% (22.6% when adjusted for dividends paid).

There is always the possibility that a stock market decline might lead to a huge number of redemptions by mutual fund shareholders. This, in turn, might start a tidal wave of selling stocks and bonds to pay the funds' redeeming shareholders, thus accelerating a decline in the securities markets. This has not yet happened on a large scale although it has occurred on individual issues. An optimistic view points out that purchases of new mutual fund shares have usually exceeded redemptions. A realistic view must acknowledge that investors might panic and liquidate.

History suggests that the average mutual fund investor holds his shares even during depressed, declining periods, meeting his emergencies with other cash resources. As the funds grow astronomically, only time will show whether the pattern of holding his shares will continue to be true of the average mutual fund investor.

7 How to Understand a Prospectus

A mutual fund prospectus is not a model of clarity but it must be factual. Because of rigid specifications by the SEC, mutual fund propectuses provide the information required by various acts of Congress. You should welcome this thoroughness and detail. After all, it will be your money that a fund invests.

All prospectuses have a title page prominently featuring this statement:

THESE SECURITIES HAVE NOT BEEN APPROVED OR DIS-APPROVED BY THE SECURITIES AND EXCHANGE COM-MISSION NOR HAS THE COMMISSION PASSED UPON THE ACCURACY OR ADEQUACY OF THIS PROSPECTUS. ANY REPRESENTATION TO THE CONTRARY IS A CRIMINAL OFFENSE.

This clearly affirms that the fund is a *private* investment company that attempts to comply with all government regulations, but that the government does not guarantee such compliance and it does not approve or disapprove of the fund's policies or objectives. Irate mutual fund shareholders have been known to hold the Federal government responsible for poor investment results or irregularities in fund management. The above statement places the responsibility

77

exactly where it belongs: on the fund itself and on the investor for his unrealistic expectations of guaranteed performance.

Determining the Per Share Cost to You

A prospectus can only tell you *how* the cost of a share is determined. This cost, called "the net asset value per share," is determined by dividing all the cash, other assets, and total current market value of all the securities in the fund portfolio by the outstanding number of shares. For example, on December 31, 1968, one fund's statement looked like this:

Net Assets (cash, assets and value of securities)	$1,195,139
Divided by shares then outstanding	235,443
Equals asset value of each share in the fund	5.08

Prospectuses give you the net asset value per share at the end of each year in the fund's history. The cost of a share to you on any given day is not found in the prospectus because of the fluctuation of the market. The daily net asset value per share of a fund is found in the financial pages of most large metropolitan newspapers, usually under the heading "Investment Trusts," (see pages 26–27). If it is a smaller fund (under 2000 shareholders), it may be carried in a "Weekly List" on Mondays in *The Wall Street Journal, The New York Times* or *Barron's*. If you have no access to these sources, a phone call to a brokerage house should help. Also, your local library may have copies that you can check.

Approaching a Prospectus

Many investors get bogged down trying to read a prospectus as though it were a novel or a short story, expecting it to inspire, delight, or otherwise stir them. Many others never bother to read a prospectus. Both of these types of investors are foolish. The purpose of a prospectus is to inform. The easiest way to find information is to know exactly what you are looking for.

Experience reveals that fund investors have questions which follow some order of importance. A study of actual prospectuses reveals that all of them contain roughly 10 to 15 sections that have a similar pattern of organization and content with slight variations in section headings and arrangement. We propose to derive an "Analysis Sheet" of questions for you to use in tracking down information in a prospectus. To develop it, we will consider the most important parts of a prospectus, section by section, providing what may be helpful comments and questions. Following are the major common sections, considered in what is probably their descending order of importance.

I. INVESTMENT GOAL AND POLICY

Easily your prime concern as an investor is the fund's *purpose*. Here the management tells you the investment policy of the fund. It may be long-range growth of your investment. It may be income. Growth, income and stability may all be mentioned. If so, some relative emphasis will be stated. What *is* the goal and what *is* the emphasis?

What is the *main type of security* in which the fund's management will usually invest? Will it be common stocks, preferred stocks with established dividend rates, or bonds? In the portfolio's diversification of securities, what will be the relative apportionments? What will be the fund's attitude toward *changing its portfolio holdings* (from common stocks to bonds, for example)? Will the policy be one of retentiveness, balanced trading, or volatile trading? How much turnover will occur within each portfolio investment category and within the fund overall?

How much risk does the management intend to take in its investment program—minimum, average, or greater than average?

Under what circumstances will the management sell securities and stocks in its portfolio? What seems to be the dominant *tone* of the investment policy statement—retentive, balanced, or volatile? This tone will become more and more evident as you read prospectuses.

II. INVESTMENT RESTRICTIONS

This is a most important section because it tells you what, under the by-laws of the fund, the fund may *not* do. Furthermore, the restrictions may not be changed without the stockholder's approval. It therefore describes the *limits* of the management's investment function and provides additional information about what happens to your money.

The list of restrictions runs anywhere from 5 to 15, and these will vary from fund to fund. Among the commonest restrictions are "short selling," which means selling a security not owned with the intention of buying it back at a lower price. "Buying on margin" is another restriction and involves buying securities by depositing a percentage of the total purchase price. Both of the preceding are highly speculative techniques. Additional restrictions may be *borrowing money, underwriting securities, buying real estate, buying commodities, investing in other funds, lending money, mortgaging fund securities, investing more than a certain percentage of the fund's assets in one industry or in one type of security.* Again, the restrictions will add up to a certain *tone* of the degree of risk in the investment policy of the fund, from the very conservative to the very speculative.

III. PER SHARE INCOME AND CAPITAL CHANGES (variously called "Condensed Financial Information," etc.)

Next to the statement of the fund's policy and investment restrictions, this is the most important section of the prospectus because it shows the fund's *performance* record throughout the fund's existence. The form is the same in every prospectus. You should become familiar with it and develop skill in studying the figures in terms of the investment policy and the type of fund.

A. Studying an Example of a Growth Fund Performance

Let us look at the performance record in the prospectus of a well-known mutual fund which we shall call the "X Growth Stock Fund, Inc." Its investment policy says, in part, "The major objectives of the Fund are to seek long-term appreciation of capital and increase of income through investment in common stocks which are believed to have favorable prospects for continued growth in earnings and dividend payments." In other words, it is a growth fund of the diversified common stocks (dcs) variety.

Here is the fund's performance for ten years. Study it carefully as you consider the questions that follow it; of course, you would also want to know how it was rated in comparison with other funds. If it was rated high, you would also want to compare its performance with the performance of other highly rated funds of its type before you make your investment decision.

Comments

Since this is primarily a growth fund, you will want to examine, first, the changes in net asset value from year to year; second, the dividend payments; and third, the earnings or realized capital gains.

(A) For growth in a share's value, what is the record? (See line 8.) From $9.22 at the end of 1957, a share's value increased to $24.57 at the end of 1967, or an increase of 167%. In the serious decline years of 1962 and 1966 the per-share-value dropped but it substantially recovered in 1963 and 1967. The pattern of share value is clearly *up*.

X Growth Stock Fund, Inc.

Per Share Income and Capital Changes

(For a share outstanding throughout the year ended December 31)

	1957	1958	1959	1960	1961	1962	1963	1964	1965	1966	1967
INCOME AND EXPENSE											
1. Income	$.33	.31	.35	.37	.37	.38	.38	.40	.46	.52	.55
2. Operating Expenses	$.09	.09	.11	.12	.13	.11	.10	.10	.10	.12	.13
3. Net Income	$.24	.22	.24	.25	.24	.27	.28	.30	.34	.40	.42
4. Dividends from Net Income	$.24	.22	.23	.25	.25	.27	.28	.30	.34	.38	.39
CAPITAL CHANGES											
5. Net Asset Value Beginning of Year	$10.19	9.22	12.15	13.70	14.15	16.89	14.23	16.30	17.60	21.16	24.67
6. Net Realized and Unrealized Gains (or Losses on Securities)	$(0.55)	3.45	2.04	.85	3.25	(2.41)	2.35	1.64	4.16	(0.58)	2.50
7. Distributions from Realized Capital Gains	$.42	.52	.50	.40	.50	.25	.28	.34	.60	.50	.53
8. Net Asset Value at End of Year	$9.22	12.15	13.70	14.15	16.89	14.23	16.30	17.60	21.16	20.10	24.57
9. Ratio of Operating Expenses to Average Net Assets	.90%	.89%	.88%	.88%	.77%	.72%	.65%	.61%	.60%	.58%	.61%
10. Ratio of Net Income to Average Net Assets	2.44%	2.09%	1.86%	1.85%	1.53%	1.90%	1.83%	1.73%	1.76%	1.97%	1.85%
11. Shares Outstanding at End of Year (,000 omitted)	1,023	1,381	2,083	2,821	4,250	5,575	6,393	7,326	9,303	12,268	15,208

(B) What is the dividend record? (See line 4.) Dividends were declared every year even in the decline periods. Furthermore, the dividend amount tended to increase each year.

(C) For capital gains distributions, each year showed a profit. (See line 7.) Again, the pattern was *up*.

Remember, to calculate your in-the-pocket return, add the dividends (line 4) and the capital gains distributions (line 7). The ratio of net income to average net assets deals only with dividends (see line 10). The ratio would be higher if capital gains distributions were also included but, by law, they cannot be stated as part of "net income."

Even if dividends and capital gains had been lower, the primary goal of the fund (growth in the net asset value per share) has been achieved. Had a shareholder taken all dividends and capital gains distributions in additional shares, the value of his investment would have increased substantially.

B. Studying an Example of an Income Fund Performance

Let us look next at the "Condensed Financial Information" section of the prospectus of a fund whose investment objective states, "The primary objectives of the fund, though their achievement cannot be assured, are to conserve the principal of the Trust and to utilize efficiently its assets for the purpose of earning regular income." In other words, it aims at income and stability (Group V, S-I: see Chapter 15). Growth is a secondary consideration.

Comments

Since this is an income fund, you will want to examine carefully the dividend performance (see line 4). Each year for all ten years

Y INCOME FUND

Per Share Income and Capital Changes

(For a share outstanding throughout the year ended December 31)

	1958	1959	1960	1961	1962	1963	1964	1965	1966	1967
INCOME AND EXPENSE										
1. Income	$.12	.13	.12	.12	.11	.10	.10	.11	.12	.12
2. Operating Expenses	.03	.03	.03	.03	.03	.02	.02	.02	.02	.02
3. Net Income	.09	.10	.09	.09	.08	.08	.08	.09	.09	.10
4. Dividends from Net Income	.09	.09	.09	.09	.08	.08	.08	.09	.10	.11
CAPITAL CHANGES										
5. Net Asset Value Beginning of Year	$2.85	3.22	3.36	2.90	3.25	2.62	2.73	2.76	2.77	2.39
6. Net Realized and Unrealized Gains (or Losses on Securities)	.55	.31	(.32)	.51	(.46)	.28	.20	.17	(.25)	.26
7. Distributions from Realized Capital Gains	.18	.18	.14	.16	.16	.17	.17	.16	.13	.09
8. Net Asset Value at End of Year	$3.22	3.36	2.90	3.25	2.62	2.73	2.76	2.77	2.39	2.55
9. Ratio of Operating Expenses to Average Net Assets	.94%	.92%	.88%	.90%	.90%	.90%	.90%	.90%	.90%	.90%
10. Ratio of New Income to Average Net Assets	2.88%	2.75%	2.81%	2.63%	2.60%	2.56%	2.57%	3.07%	3.92%	3.77%
11. Shares Outstanding at End of Year (,000 omitted)	3,050	3,391	3,614	3,503	3,675	3,860	4,028	4,113	4,369	4,406

the dividend has held to 8¢, 9¢, or 10¢ a share, rising to 11¢ in 1967. Remember that 1962 and 1966 were market decline years. In percentages the dividend was from between 2.88% and 3.77%, even rising a bit in 1966 (see line 10).

For actual in-the-pocket return, add the capital gains distributions (line 7) to dividends from net income (line 4). In other words, for the entire period, a shareholder received every year between 20¢ and 30¢ per share in-the-pocket return or about 8% in the best years (27 cents in 1958 and 1959) and close to 8% in the worst year (20 cents in 1967).

The net asset value per share at the end of each year remained fairly constant for the first two years, dropped in 1960, rose in 1961, dropped a bit in 1962 and has remained fairly level since (see line 8). The net asset value per share did not grow, *but growth was not the goal of the fund.*

If you had wanted a fairly steady 8% return (dividends plus capital gains distributions), this fund would have been one to consider. Of course, you would want to compare this fund with other income funds to see whether the annual return was as consistent, but higher than the 8% earned by the first fund. (Note that the fund's number of shares increased (line 11) from about 3 million to almost 4½ million. Note also that operating expenses (line 9) held fairly well to a bit under 1% annually.)

Remember that, by themselves, performance figures in the prospectus of a fund are insufficient data to use in deciding on an investment. You must *compare the figures of two or more similar types of funds.* It is recommended that the figures of at least six highly-rated funds be compared before an investment decision is made.

IV. PURCHASE OF SHARES (variously called "Sale of Shares," "Offering Price and Conditions," "Net Asset Value and Offering Price," etc.)

After explaining how the price of a share is determined, this section will give you the per-share sales charge. A table shows how the sales charge drops as the amount invested rises. Many funds state that if you sign a "letter of intent" to purchase shares in excess of a certain dollar amount within a given time (say $15,000 within 13 months), you can receive the benefit of the reduced sales charge.

Do not confuse the letter of intent (which is designed to decrease the sales charges on your purchase) with the contractual front-end load (which carries a higher sales charge during the first year). The letter of intent is *not* a contract whereas the contractual plan requires your compliance with the terms of the agreement.

Also, some funds have "Right of Accumulation" features. In these funds, whenever the net asset value of your account exceeds one of the reduced sales charge breakpoints, subsequent amounts invested in your account will receive the reduced sales charge. Do not confuse these rights with either the letter of intent or features of contractual plans.

In this section of the prospectus you will find the required initial investment and through whom you must invest (any broker, a particular broker, or the fund itself). There are a great variety of share purchase plans, ranging from "open" accounts that allow any amount of money (as little as $10) at any time, to a required initial minimum and a subsequent minimum each time you invest. Some funds require a substantial initial minimum ($1,000 to $25,-000), with lower minimums for each subsequent purchase. You should be sure that you understand the *required* and the *allowable* initial and subsequent investments. Confusion, disappointment and unbalanced family budgets have resulted for investors who blindly bought into a fund without being able either to maintain a required pace of investments or who overinvested without realizing that smaller, more moderate purchases were both possible and desirable.

Most prospectuses are accompanied by an application blank for share purchases. It bears careful reading. Before signing, be sure that you understand the type of account you are starting. Is the plan voluntary (open account) and subject to change at your will? You may want to avoid a front-end load (contractual) plan, described in Chapter 2, in which a large part of your first year's purchases may go for sales commissions. An enthusiastic broker may give you different advice. Many investors have had sad experiences with such plans.

V. REDEMPTION OF SHARES (variously called "Repurchase of Shares," "Liquidation of Shares," etc.)

No mutual fund can legally refuse to redeem shares. The fund must honor a request for redemption within seven days except during a period when the New York Stock Exchange is closed, or the SEC (by order) permits temporary suspension of redemptions, or an emergency exists as defined by the SEC.

The redemption of shares can be time-consuming and involves the possibility of loss in net asset value between the time redemption is requested and the time that it is actually accomplished. Also, depending on your temperament, redemption requirements may also be annoyingly detailed and irritating unless you know exactly what to expect. First, most funds require a written request to the fund, directly or through a broker, which will be honored according to the net asset value of a share at the close of the day on which the request is received. Some funds may accept a telegram, a phone call or a personal visit. So far, so good, but now it may get sticky.

The stickiness is tied up with share certificates. Every fund has what it calls a "custodian," which is a bank that holds your share certificates in safe keeping unless you have them issued in your name at the time of purchase. Funds stress this as a convenience. Apparently, most people prefer it that way instead of keeping their own certificates in a safety deposit box. Now, what do you do if the second requirement is to send the share certificate(s), "duly executed," which means properly filled out with signatures guaranteed by a bank official? The date that the redemption request will be honored may *not* be the date that the request is received by the fund, *but* the date that the request *and* the share certificate(s) are received.

You may have to write to the custodian bank, request your share certificates, wait for them to arrive in the mail, get them executed and return them to the fund with your request for redemption. The variations on this theme may be numerous, depending on the fund. Each fund has its own procedures. Since the larger funds may be slower, you should carefully check your understanding of the redemption procedure with your broker or by a letter to the fund.

If you are impatient with potential delays in share redemption, and if the redemption procedure described in the prospectus suggests that such delays are quite possible, you may be wise to consider a request that share certificates be sent when your first investment is made and for each successive investment thereafter. The price of a safety deposit box could be worth it. On the other hand, most people feel that it is very impractical to accumulate reams of share certificates, some of which may be fractions of shares representing dividend or capital gains distributions which were used to buy additional shares.

Some "low-load" or "no-load" funds have a redemption fee of 1%. Most funds have none. Some large management companies that sponsor three or four different mutual funds will charge an investor a flat $5.00 fee for switching assets from one fund to another. Many companies do not have a conversion feature.

In summary, you should not fear a fund's ability to redeem your shares but you should know what the redemption procedure is by reading the prospectus carefully. You should plan accordingly.

VI. DIVIDENDS AND CAPITAL GAINS

The importance of this section of a prospectus is indicated by two questions that you are likely to want answered: first, "When are dividends declared?" second, "How do I get them?" You should always remember that dividends and capital gains are declared only *after* all expenses of the fund are deducted from the year's profits.

Many funds declare dividends yearly; some declare them quarterly. They will send cash if requested. With the exception of the income funds, they will usually urge that dividends be reinvested automatically. Unless you specify that you want the dividends in cash when you make out your share purchase application, a fund will automatically reinvest them in additional shares. Some funds *require* that you take your dividends as reinvestments.

The above generalizations about dividends also apply to capital gains distributions except that capital gains distributions are declared annually. Remember that a capital gain represents a "return of capital." Nevertheless, as an in-the-pocket return, you ought to add it to the dividend to calculate your investment return. Ordinarily, certificates for shares acquired through reinvestment of dividends and capital gains will *not* be issued unless you specifically make the request on your initial share purchase application.

A third question frequently asked by investors is, "Why shouldn't I make a substantial investment a few days before the dividends and capital gains are declared and thereby enjoy a windfall?" The answer is that all dividends and capital gains distributions received shortly after the purchase of shares in a fund reduce the net asset value of the shares by the amount of the dividend or capital gains distribution. Furthermore, although in effect a return of capital, the capital gains distributions and dividends are subject to Federal income tax.

Read this prospectus section carefully to understand when dividends and capital gains distributions are declared, and in what form they *may* or *must* be taken.

VII. FEDERAL TAX STATUS (variously called "Taxes," "Tax Treatment," "Tax Status," etc.)

Many shareholders do not understand that most mutual funds pay no income taxes. A careful reading of this section of a prospectus will call your attention to the fact that if the fund wants to qualify as a regulated investment company, it must distribute at least 90% of its net income to its shareholders. Furthermore, the fund can only be taxed on those capital gains which it does not distribute to its shareholders. As a result, the usual policy of the fund is to distribute substantially *all* its net income and net realized capital gains. You, the shareholder, will pay the income taxes.

On your mutual fund dividends you are allowed *one* deduction: $100 on the dividends received by each shareholder. A man and wife filing a joint return may therefore claim $200 of their dividends as tax deductible. This favorably compares with the "no deduction allowable" for interest paid by your bank, your credit union or your savings and loan association.

No deductions can be claimed for capital gains distributions. Most funds will send you an annual report with information about dividends and capital gains distributions paid during the year. They will provide instructions about the portion of each payment which should be reported by you as a dividend and the portion which should be reported as a long-term capital gain.

Several accountants have indicated that there have been mutual fund shareholders who did *not* report income dividends and capital gains distributions when taken as reinvestments in additional shares. The shareholders mistakenly believed that unless they received the dividends and capital gains distributions as cash-in-the-pocket, they did not have to report them. "Unrealized capital gains" on the increase of asset value on their original shares are not taxable until the shares are redeemed.

This section will also tell you if the fund offers the Keogh plan (HR-10) for a self-employed individual. Under this plan, you may delay payment of taxes on dividends and capital gains distributions. Payment of taxes will fall due when you retire. A small annual fee (usually $5.00) is charged by the fund's custodian for the required bookkeeping.

VIII. MANAGEMENT, INVESTMENT ADVISOR COMPANY, UNDER-WRITER, AND BROKERAGE ALLOCATION.

These four sections in a prospectus need to be distinguished from each other carefully, yet the four taken together account for a fund's major operating expenses, which must be paid before dividends and capital gains distributions are paid. Further, some of the alleged abuses in the mutual fund industry are often pinpointed here.

A. *Management.* The Management consists of the officers and the directors of a fund. They make the *final* decisions about securities that shall be bought and sold in the fund's portfolio, when to invest, and when to remain in a cash position. Some or all of them may be salaried and they may hold shares in the fund. Their names, past occupations, and fund holdings are detailed in the prospectus.

B. *Investment Advisor* (variously called "Management Company," etc.). This is the company that, under a contract with the fund, *advises* the officers and directors about what investments to make and also what proportion of a fund's assets to hold in cash. The investment advisor's fee is usually ½ of 1% a year which may be reduced if fund assets exceed a stated amount. None of this fee is passed on to brokers or dealers. Under the contract, the investment advisor usually pays all executive salaries, executive expenses, office rent, sales commissions, and promotion expenses in connection with the distribution of fund shares. Income received by the investment advisor from the sales charge is passed on almost entirely to dealers and brokers or spent on advertising.

Sometimes a member of the investment advisor may also be an officer or a director of the fund's management. Sometimes the investment advisor and the management are one and the same. The prospectus will identify the investment advisor and its arrangements with the fund.

C. *Underwriter*. The shares of a mutual fund are distributed by the underwriter. Sometimes the underwriter is a completely separate company that specializes in promoting and distributing a fund's shares. Sometimes the underwriter is the same company as the investment advisor.

D. *Brokerage Allocation*. When the fund's management buys and sells securities, it does so through brokers, paying the usual brokerage fee. Some prospectuses will state that management attempts to allocate brokerage business to those firms that will help sell the fund's shares and that offer the fund broad investment analysis services. This is called "reciprocity business" and the brokerage fees received by the fund sales organization are known as "reciprocals." Other funds make no such statement. The prospectus will clarify the brokerage arrangement.

By now it should be clear that overlaps, special interests, interlocking directorates and favoritism may exist among these four administrative elements in a fund. Such relationships can lead to abuses, excesses and irregularities, just as they do in government, education and other businesses. In most of the funds there is neither collusion nor illegality. Critics of the funds are quick to spot any questionable practices so the industry works hard to police itself. Its record is good. Under the surveillance of government, the fund industry will probably continue its efforts at self-regulation.

A careful reading of the prospectus will clarify for you the fund's management relationships. Remember, too, that these four administrative elements account for the fund's operating expenses. You will do well to carefully consider the amount of these costs in comparing funds because the costs are deducted before any dividends and capital gains distributions are made.

IX. Financial Statement

Every prospectus contains a detailed financial statement of the fund's assets. You should know the total net asset value of a fund under consideration and, if possible, the cash flow of the fund. When a fund moves beyond the $500,000,000 asset figure, it may be getting unwieldy in its investment techniques (there have been notable exceptions) and you may do well to consider a smaller fund whose performance is similar. An investor already in a fund should also consider diversifying his holdings rather than remaining exclusively in a big fund. Too few investors know the asset size of funds that they are considering. The financial statement provides easy access to this figure, although, with the phenomenal growth of funds today, it may have changed dramatically in two or three months. Easily spotted, too, is a statement of liabilities.

Another revealing figure is the amount of cash on hand in relation to the total net assets. The greater the cash assets of the fund at any given time (annually or quarterly), the less promising the fund's management apparently felt the market to be for investments at that time. Here you can also find a statement of the income and expenses of the fund for the preceding year. Specifically listed are the expenses and the *ratio of the total operating expenses to total investment income*. This is the kind of information that any efficiently run household wants to know. Should you want less?

Finally, in these statements each fund is required to give the "Changes in Net Assets" for the prior *three years*. You can quickly spot the fund's recent record for growth, for making a profit, and for retaining its shareholders by studying annual figures on (a) the net assets; (b) the number of shares issued and redeemed; (c) the net income dividends per share; and (d) the capital gains distributions per share. While you may not be able to interpret these figures with professional skill, you can certainly raise intelligent questions for a broker to answer.

X. STATEMENT OF INVESTMENTS (variously called "Portfolio Holdings," "Statement of Securities and Cash Owned," "Investments," etc.)

Here you can take a long, hard look at the industries, companies, bonds and notes in which the fund was invested as of the prospectus date. You can learn how much of each security is owned and the percentage of the total portfolio that it represents. You can sometimes see what the securities cost the fund and what their value was at the end of the year. Some investors are pleasantly surprised at discovering the degree to which their dollars are invested in well-known companies.

To the extent that your fund is invested in well-known common stocks, to that extent will the daily net asset value of your shares often reflect the daily increase or decrease of stock prices generally. To the extent that your fund is heavily invested in less well-known, speculative stocks, to that extent may the daily net asset value of your shares fluctuate more widely than the general market movement. Finally, to the extent that your fund is invested in preferred stocks and bonds, to that extent may the daily net asset value of your shares remain stable.

XI. VOTING RIGHTS (cumulative or noncumulative)

You will either have cumulative or noncumulative voting rights in the fund(s) in which you invest. The differences between these methods is not usually of urgent concern. However, you may wish to note which method is used for your own satisfaction. Be sure to check the prospectus for this information.

We have considered most of the principal sections of a mutual fund prospectus. The two exceptions are *Investment Plans* and *Withdrawal Plans* which will be taken up in greater detail in Chapters 11 and 12.

We are now ready to suggest an "Analysis Form" to use in studying, analyzing, and selecting a fund, or for keeping well-informed about a fund in which you may already own shares. A broker may help you find the answers if you cannot do it on your own. The answers will give an over-all profile of a fund and will expedite comparisons among funds of the same type.

MUTUAL FUND ANALYSIS SHEET

The _____ Fund
Prospectus Date _____

I. INVESTMENT GOAL & POLICY
   a. What is the primary and the secondary goal? (Growth _____ Income _____ Stability _____)
   b. What is the main type of security in which the fund invests? _____
   c. What is the fund's stated policy concerning portfolio changes? _____
   d. What investment restrictions has the fund adopted, and which are emphasized? _____

II. ADMINISTRATION
   a. How many shares are owned by members of the Board of Directors? _____
   b. Is the fund internally or externally managed? _____
   c. Who is the investment advisor? _____
   d. What is the investment advisor's fee? _____ Is it subject to change? _____ When may it be changed? _____
   e. Are any members of the investment advisor also members of the Board of Directors? _____ If so, how many? _____
   f. What fund expenses does the investment advisor pay? _____

g. What company is the underwriter or distributor of fund shares?_____
h. How is it related to the investment advisor? _____
i. Does the fund allocate its brokerage in any particular manner? _____
_____ How much was paid the preceding year in
brokerage commissions? _____

III. ASSETS OF THE FUND

	a	b	c	d
1 Year				
5 Years				
10 Years				
15 Years				
20 Years				
1962				
1966				

a. *Amount* of increase or decrease in total fund assets.
b. *Percentage* of increase or decrease in total fund assets.
c. *Amount* of increase or decrease in net asset value per share.
d. *Percentage* of increase or decrease in net asset value per share.

1. If net asset value per share decreased in 1962 and 1966, how rapidly
   did it recover to its pre-decline price level?

	1 mo.	3 mos.	6 mos.	12 mos.	15 mos.	18 mos.	Longer
1962							
1966							

2. How much has the net asset value per share changed since the latest
   prospectus was published? _____%
3. What proportion of the holdings of the fund is in bonds (_____%)
   preferred stocks (_____%) common stocks (_____%) notes
   (_____%) cash (_____%)?
4. In which industries does the fund invest heavily? _____
5. What is the current portfolio turnover rate? _____% per year
6. How much of the fund's net annual income is distributed to shareowners? _____%

IV. DIVIDENDS AND CAPITAL GAINS DISTRIBUTIONS

a. What were the dividends and capital gains distributions each year?

Year	Dividends	C.G.D.	Total	Year	Dividends	C.G.D.	Total
1954				1964			
1955				1965			

1956	____	____	____	1966	____	____	____
1957	____	____	____	1967	____	____	____
1958	____	____	____	1968	____	____	____
1959	____	____	____	1969	____	____	____
1960	____	____	____	1970	____	____	____
1961	____	____	____	1971	____	____	____
1962	____	____	____	1972	____	____	____
1963	____	____	____	1973	____	____	____

b. What were the *average* annual dividends? (add all dividends, divide by number of years). $_____

c. What were the *average* annual capital gains distributions? $_____

d. What was the *average* annual total return (dividends plus capital gains distributions all added up and divided by the number of years). $_____

e. Did the dividends and capital gains distributions follow a general pattern of *increase* or *decrease?* _____

f. In what years were dividends and/or capital gains distributions below average? Dividends _____ Capital Gains _____

g. On what dates are dividends and capital gains distributions paid? Dividend Dates _____ Capital Gains Distributions Dates _____

h. What is the procedure for handling dividends and capital gains distributions?

	May Be Taken in Cash	May Be Reinvested	Must Be Reinvested
Capital Gains Dist.	_____	_____	_____
Dividends	_____	_____	_____

V. PURCHASE OF SHARES

a. What is the sales charge? _____% At what amounts does it decrease, and to what % of the investment? _____

b. Are rights of accumulation included in the sales charge computations? _____

c. What are the minimum purchases?

	Initial	Monthly	Quarterly	Semi-Annual	Annual	Total
In Dollars	____	____	____	____	____	____
In Shares	____	____	____	____	____	____

d. If your purchase is under a contractual plan, what amount of your first annual investment will go toward the sales charge? $_____

e. What type of Keogh plan is available for self-employed individuals? Pension _____ Profit sharing _____.

f. How are certificates handled? (Held by custodian bank _____) (Issued to shareowner _____) (Optional with investor _____)

VI. REDEMPTION OF SHARES

a. How must redemption be handled? (Duly executed certificates _____) (Signed stock power sufficient _____) (Notification of fund by mail _____)

b. At what net asset value will the fund redeem your shares? (Same day request received _____) (Same day executed certificates received _____) (Same day stock power received _____)

c. What is the redemption fee, if any? _____

8 The Acquisition Charge in Mutual Funds

When you make out your check for $1,000 to purchase shares in a mutual fund (let's say for 50 shares at $20 a share), the usual 8½% sales charge or "load" will come to $85. Nine hundred and fifteen dollars will go to work for you in the fund. The 8½% sales charge will go in three directions: 2% to the underwriter, 6½% to the dealer who then pays the broker from 3% to 4% in commission. That 8½% of the offering price is equal to 9.3% of the amount actually invested for you. The SEC thought that this was unnecessarily high and so did former President Johnson. The United States Senate Banking Committee believes that you are being overcharged, as do a number of financial experts.

On the other hand, in one of his daily columns, Donald White (former financial editor of *The San Francisco Examiner*) recently observed, "If you want to see what a case of mass apoplexy looks like, drop into the office of any brokerage house that does a big business in mutual funds . . . Mutual fund brokers and their bosses are livid over a Senate Committee proposal that could well become law—that would drastically cut the present eight to nine percent sales charge on mutual fund purchases."

Your investment dollar is the center of this bitter controversy. In trying to make an investment decision, remember that the word "load" is synonymous with "sales charge" and nothing else. It is the cost of *acquiring* shares in a fund. It has nothing to do with the *cost of managing* your investment. Unfortunately, the word "load" has acquired negative connotations which can confuse you in your investment decision.

Background of the Controversy on Load

In 1940 Congress passed the Investment Company Act which regulated the mutual fund industry, at that time representing about $500 million in assets. Congress recognized that if the funds grew, the law might have to be renewed. The funds did grow, dramatically. The Securities and Exchange Commission decided that the 1940 Act needed re-evaluation and called on the Wharton School of Finance to study the industry. The Wharton Report appeared in 1962. It was followed by a Special Study of the Securities Markets for the SEC. In December, 1966, the SEC issued a report on the "Public Policy Implications of Investment Company Growth," in which SEC Chairman Manuel F. Cohen called mutual fund sales charges "excessive." There came next a bill drafted by the Senate Banking Committee, hotly debated in 1967 and 1968, that would have reduced the permissible maximum sales charges from 9% to 5%. The Senate passed this bill, which later died in the House of Representatives.

In June, 1968, legislation was passed leaving it up to the mutual fund industry to regulate itself by reducing sales charges through the National Association of Securities Dealers. Final power was vested in the watchdog SEC to fix sales charges if it disagreed with the industry's determination. The issue is crucial. How it will be resolved remains the great question that will continue haunting the industry. A complete critical analysis of the various arguments would require a book devoted exclusively to this subject.*

* If you want cogent, persuasive arguments in dialogue style given by in-

What Does the Mutual Fund Industry Say?

Let us consider the industry's views and some of its answers to criticisms of the sales charge as "excessive." First, the fund industry insists that the government is going too far if it tries to tell the funds how to price their products. This is the perennial conflict between two different philosophies—one saying that free enterprise is best qualified to decide on standards of equity and fairness, the other, that government has the right and the obligation to define and enforce fairness in economic transactions.

Second, the fund industry flatly rejects the description of present loads as "excessive," insisting that it is based on an invalid comparison of the sales charges on stock trading with the sales charges for mutual funds. For example, small lot sales charges on the New York Stock Exchange are $100 to $399, 2% plus $3; $400 to $2,399, 1% plus $7; $3,400 to $4,999, ½% plus $19; $5,000 and over, $\frac{1}{10}$% plus $39. Fund spokesmen maintain that a share in a mutual fund represents a diversified group of securities which, if bought individually in small lots, would cost the investor much more than the 8½% commission for a mutual fund share. Furthermore, they point out that you pay a sales charge when you sell an individual stock as well as when you buy it. In contrast, most mutual funds charge no redemption fee.

Third, fund representatives insist that mutual funds are very different from other securities because they cannot be placed on the shelf, side by side with listed securities. Mutual funds are unique. They are sold differently from other securities. Also, a variety of

---

telligent and reasonable members of government, industry, and higher education, refer to the University of Pennsylvania Law School's *Conference on Mutual Funds*, the *University of Pennsylvania Law Review*, Vol. 115, No. 5, March, 1967. This is an absorbing, readable, and valuable record in which the load, front-end load, and management fee controversies are discussed.

services are built into mutual funds, including the following: professional management, diversification, guaranteed redemption, reinvestment of dividends and capital gains distributions, accumulation plans, withdrawal plans, letters of intent, cumulative discounts, exchange privileges, custodian arrangements, and bookkeeping conveniences.

Fourth, the mutual funds claim that the SEC and other critics completely ignore the way in which mutual funds are marketed as compared with listed or over-the-counter stocks. Individual securities are usually sold by brokers over the telephone or to regular customers. This makes for high volume but it also makes for a low cost in each transaction. In contrast, when selling funds, a broker must canvass for investors, counsel the prospective buyer and spend valuable time doing follow-up work. One mutual fund executive claims that a broker must make ten phone calls to generate three appointments from which he may make one sale. The chairman of one mutual fund management estimates that the average broker puts in about 20 hours per sale, thus requiring a sales charge high enough to compensate him for the many prospects who do not buy.

Fifth, the funds argue that the sales charge is justified not only by the initial advice and guidance you receive from the broker but also by the periodic counseling you receive about your fund holdings and estate planning. Why, ask the funds, shouldn't a broker reap the reward for this expertise? Three percent or 4% commission is hardly excessive for such readily available investment counsel.

Sixth, the industry asks, "What is so sacred about the 5% sales charge which the SEC recommends?" It appears to the funds as a completely arbitrary, almost capricious selection with no economic basis to support it. Furthermore, the fund industry believes that it can document the very real dangers of a 5% sales charge as a figure which could greatly harm dealers and brokers. A 1967 study by the National Association of Securities Dealers claimed that the proposed cut of the sales charge to 5% would force small broker-dealer firms (those with gross income of less than $2.5 million) into a 50% reduction of profits. The income of larger firms would drop by about 8%. These figures assume not only a reduction of sales charges but also of commissions paid to dealers by fund managers in exchange for selling fund shares or giving other investment advisory services to the fund.

Seventh, industry spokesmen predict that cutting the sales charge will significantly reduce sales. A point could be reached where redemptions exceed new capital flowing into the fund. This loss of assets could lead to a declining portfolio. The management of a declining portfolio can be more difficult than the management of a growing one. The per-share cost of management would probably increase as total assets declined. Since investors pay the management fee, it follows that cutting sales charges will increase the proportionate expenses for shareholders.

Eighth, the SEC contends that the present sales charge maximum of 9% eliminates competition among funds, so that the investor presumably has no knowledge of alternative kinds of investments (such as closed-end funds, no-load funds, and other securities). The fund industry claims that even if this were true, it would not make much difference to investors, because it is professional management and diversification that they are buying. Also, the human habit of failing to overcome inertia is an enemy of the do-it-yourself investor. Even if such investors knew about no-loads, closed-end funds, and other securities, they would probably still do nothing. Most investors have no realistic alternatives because of their own limitations in time and experience. Even if they decided to invest in stock with small amounts of money, the odds are high that they would buy some low-priced, over-the-counter security and risk substantial losses.

What Do the Critics of the Mutual Fund Industry Say?

In its "Public Policy" report two years ago, the SEC acknowl-edged that the mutual fund industry could be proud of its record, that it had fulfilled an important public need, and that it had earned a place as an important member of the nation's financial commu-nity. The SEC also stated that, on the whole, mutual funds were well-managed; nevertheless, it had some sharp criticisms which are echoed by others.

First, some critics contend that current commission rates have led to the overselling of mutual funds. The lure of sales profits has galvanized brokers to push people into mutual funds when they might be better off investing in other kinds of securities. When the funds contend that cutting their commission rates would decrease their sales efforts, critics say, "Good, you ought to. Your growth is unnatural and dangerous."

In the same vein, these critics charge that current mutual fund commissions are a powerful incentive to irresponsible elements who do irreparable harm to investors. The SEC report stated that registration figures indicate about one broker for every 70 mutual fund shareholders. Considering the recent growth of the funds, the ratio today may be even smaller. By any yardstick, SEC Chairman Cohen insisted, this is a top-heavy and oversized distribution sys-tem. Mr. Cohen also estimated that up to 70% of the brokers were part-timers and that the turnover was high. The benefits of skill, knowledge, and experience needed by investors are bound to be diluted by fly-by-night hucksters.

Third, some critics allege that current sales charges promote what is called "perverse price competition." Some funds, with their own sales forces, will compete with each other to attract investors. Most funds, on the other hand, will make their sales through deal-ers. The dealer, it is said, will look for the product that will give him the biggest profit. So he and his brokers will favor those funds which will give them the biggest sales commission and consequently cost the investor the most money.

Fourth, the SEC believes that comparing a purchase of shares in a mutual fund with the purchase of stock through the stock exchange is a valid comparison. Both are investment transactions. But the SEC insists that it is not fair of the funds' defenders to compare the higher cost of buying a large number of securities in small lots with the lower cost of buying mutual fund shares. The cost of purchasing the stock is paid by the investor through the fund's brokerage fee, while brokerage houses on the Stock Exchange bear part of the cost of buying stock for a client. The SEC does not state how much "churning" is done in individual stocks to generate sales commissions, an action which is specifically prohibited by the "Statement of Policy" of the SEC when mutual fund shares are involved.

Fifth, a sympathetic view of the 5% sales charge recommended by the SEC holds that it is neither arbitrary nor capricious but fair and reasonable compared with the 8½% to 9% which these viewers believe to be unreasonable. The SEC never claimed "excess profits" or "overcompensation" were being made by dealers or brokers. Its focus was a comparison between sales charges on exchange-listed securities (including closed-end mutual funds) and on mutual fund shares. Both types of transactions are not so different as to justify the difference between stock exchange commission rates and mutual fund sales charges, according to the SEC.

The SEC gave an example of $200 put into a fund at an 8½% charge. This cost was 40% more than a purchase and a sale of similar size in a listed stock costing $40 a share. The mutual fund load remained the same until the first breaking point, usually $12,-500, when it dropped to 7.5%, while the stock exchange commission declined at a faster rate. The gap between the two kinds of sales charges increased as the amount of money involved increased.

The SEC calculated that a $4,000 fund purchase cost 4.76 times the in-and-out commission on a stock exchange transaction. This is based on a single transaction, however, and does not take into consideration the annual number of trades made by investors.

Sixth, fund critics claim that sales of mutual fund shares do not take place under competitive conditions. Competition is supposed to reduce costs to a purchaser, but it is alleged that the only competition here is among underwriters for dealer favor, "the perverse price competition" mentioned earlier. If the prospectus of Fund X says that the sales charge shall be 8½%, Section 22(d) of the Investment Company Act says that every dealer must sell the shares at that rate. This is true even though a particular dealer may think he can make an adequate profit by selling at a 5% markup while another dealer may believe that he cannot profit on less than a 10% markup. In a free market, the market would set the price. However, the SEC recommended changing the maximum sales charge to 5% rather than amending the law and freeing competitive forces, because of "the unsettling and unforeseeable effects which abolition of retail price maintenance might have on broker-dealer relationships."

Finally, some critics also point out that mutual fund shares are usually long-term investments involving portfolio turnover. Turnover costs money and it is the shareholder who pays that bill.

This smoldering issue of fund sales charges and expenses will doubtless erupt again in 1969. Government action is inevitable if the fund industry does not move in a direction satisfactory to the SEC; yet, within the fund industry itself, diverse views exist and must be reconciled. With insurance companies and large merchandising organizations moving into the mutual fund business (and savings and loan companies and banks clamoring to get in, too), can the industry agree on new, lower fund sales charges? And, if it does, will it survive as an industry or be taken over as an adjunct of banks and insurance companies? Some feel strongly that funds should be kept independent of monopolistic control.

Should You Get Into a Load Fund?

There are two bases on which you can make a decision. The first is philosophical. If, on the basis of arguments that you have read, your own experience, your own standards of "fair and reasonable" sales charges, or your own temperament and personality, you think that the average load of 8½% is too high, stay away from a load fund. Avoid the anxiety, frustration, and indignation that may lead you angrily to lock horns with your broker if your investment does not make up the sales charge in what you consider a reasonable amount of time.

If the philosophical argument is of no interest or concern to you, the second basis that you can use for a decision is a *practical* one. You can ask, "Is there an alternative to the load fund? If so, will I get a better deal?" To the first question the answer is "yes." No-load funds are available. Before you can answer the second question, you must understand what no-load funds are. Then, you must consider their record to determine if they are, in general, better bargains than load funds.

9　The No-Load Funds

One of the major developments in the mutual fund industry is the growth of no-load funds. No sales charge of any kind is made for the acquisition of shares. That fact, coupled with the outstanding performance of some no-load funds in 1967 and 1968, has made them a hoped-for "land of milk and honey." Like most apparently simple stories, this one is complex.

Common Misconceptions of No-Load Funds

Several prevalent but erroneous ideas about no-load funds need to be dispelled if one is to make intelligent investment decisions.

1. "A no-load fund gives an investor something for nothing." No-load fund managers make no such claim. Like every other fund manager, they make their money from a management fee. That fee is usually ½ of 1% of the net asset value of the fund although some are as large as 1%. Load-fund management does receive money from sales charges but passes the bulk of such charges on to dealers and brokers in the way of commissions. The remainder is usually assigned to the underwriter and custodian bank for performance of their services.

A no-load fund ordinarily sells its shares through the mail. It does not use dealers or brokers. It is no reflection on no-load funds to say that they do not give you something for nothing. No fund does, nor should you expect it to.

2. "No-load funds are no different from load funds except that they are 8½% cheaper." This is a half truth which, carelessly used, obscures the whole truth. By definition, because the no-load fund has no sales charge, it *is* cheaper in one category of acquisition costs. That it is 8½% cheaper in *all* categories of cost can only be established by examining data on other costs such as management fees, operating expenses, and redemption fees.

3. "No-load funds must have some special talent for making money which enables them to forego a sales charge." The main thing a no-load fund foregoes is a sales force; therefore, no sales charge is made. Only the record can demonstrate whether no-load fund managers have a special talent for making profits for their investors.

The three false notions above cannot be attributed to the managers of no-load funds, but originate in the grandiose hopes of the unseasoned investor.

Is a No-Load Fund a Bargain?

Easily the major criterion to use in selecting a fund is its past performance, though even that is no guarantee of future showing. While no-load funds are less expensive to acquire, an equally important question is, "Do no-load funds generally perform better than load funds?" Common sense dictates that your choice of a fund should be based on the investment objective and equality in value (not equality in cost) if the choice is not to be unrealistic. If an 8½% load fund gives you a 17% annual compounding on your investment and a no-load fund gives you a 7½% annual compounding, which is the bargain? On the other hand, if a no-load investment compounds at 12% a year and an 8½% load fund compounds at 16% a year, which is the bargain?

Comparing Load and No-Load Fund Performance

A. The Wharton Report

The most detailed study of mutual fund performance ever made was that by the Wharton School of Finance of the University of Pennsylvania, in response to a request by the SEC. Published in 1962, it was a compilation of statistical analyses of mutual funds in terms of their structure, control, growth, investment policies, performance, impact on the stock market, relationships with portfolio companies, and relationship to their investment advisors. It was prefaced by a 36-page statement of "Summary and Conclusions" by its four authors. For degree of objectivity, documentation, and thoroughness, the Wharton Report is considered the most definitive study of its kind. However, not all of its conclusions and implications would be concurred in by fund spokesmen and financial analysts.

That part of the report dealing with the performance of funds had one section which considered the relation between sales charges and cumulative performance in the period 1952–1958. Of 178 funds studied, 18 were no-load. The report listed end results and averages only. It did not name individual funds nor did it individually rank their performance. It covered only growth in the value of an investment. The major conclusion concerning the impact of sales charges on performance of a fund was this: *There is no relation between the sales charges and the performance of a fund.*

B. The FundScope Study

Each January *FundScope* publishes a study of the comparative performance of load and no-load funds. Titled, "Are No-Load

Funds a Bargain? Are Load Funds Expensive?" the article discusses the advisability of selecting a fund solely on the load charge. In vivid visual format the magazine presents statistical data to help an investor compare the performance of load and no-load funds.

The January, 1968, article[1] compared the performance of 260 individual funds of which 38 (about 15%) were no-load. Some of the 38 no-load funds charged a 1% redemption fee; others reserved the right to charge a redemption fee though none had done so up to that date. Nine of the 260 funds charged a commission ranging from 1% to 4.15%.

Performance Results Must Be Based on Appropriate Comparisons. FundScope correctly pointed out that in determining the performance of a fund, past results can be misleading. For example, if you compare the growth of a no-load fund which stresses *stability* with the growth of a load fund which stresses *growth,* your conclusion based on such a comparison will be misleading. Results are usually viewed in terms of three major investment objectives. You will have one, or a combination of these three: 1) capital appreciation; 2) price stability; 3) income. *FundScope* therefore calculated the comparative performance of load and no-load funds for growth in rising market periods, for stability in declining market periods, and for income in all periods.[2]

[1] Data from the January, 1969, issue was not available as of the writing of this book.
[2] The total number of funds that figure in rankings and ratings may vary among the 1, 5, and 10-year periods because some funds were not in existence for the full period.

Growth

One-Year Growth Performance Comparisons Between Load and No-Load Funds (1967)

From September, 1966, to September, 1967, the best performing growth fund was a load fund. Of the top-performing 25 funds, one was a no-load and 24 were load. Among the poorest-performing funds, three were no-load and 22 were load. Of the 38 no-load funds compared, 14 (about 39%) performed above average and 22 (about 61%) performed below average. One year is considered unrepresentative in measuring mutual fund performance but it can be suggestive.

5-Year Growth Performance Comparisons Between Load and No-Load Funds (1963–1967)

The top-performing fund, a no-load, had a liquidating value of $21,097 at the end of five years, based on a $10,000 lump-sum investment with all distributions reinvested. Among the top 25 performers 8 were no-load and 17 were load. Among the 25 poorest performers 2 were no-load and 23 were load. A large number of the 260 funds did not furnish 5-year data, so the 5-year statistics may not be representative. The available statistics favor the no-load funds, however. While no-loads represented 15% of the 260 funds, 32% of the top 25 performers were no-loads. Comparatively, 85% of the 260 funds were load, representing 68% of the top-performing 25.

10-Year Growth Performance Comparisons Between Load and No-Load Funds (1957–1966)

The top-performing fund, a load fund, had a liquidating value of $49,184 based on a $10,000 lump-sum investment with all distributions reinvested. If, on January 1, 1957, you had invested $10,-000 in each of the top five no-load growth funds and reinvested all dividends and capital gains distributions, ten years later (December, 1966) their *average* liquidating value would have been $28,-465. Their *combined* liquidation value would have been $142,325. If you had chosen the five top-performing load funds, investing the same amounts in the same manner, their average liquidating value at the end of the same ten years would have been $37,886. Their combined liquidation value would have been $189,431.

In these results, all costs including sales commission (if any) and redemption fee (if any) would have been deducted. These figures confirm the findings of the Wharton Report: *there is no correlation between the existence of sales charges and performance results.* These performance results were achieved in rising market periods. Had you required conservation of capital, how did the loads and the no-loads compare in price stability in declining markets?

Stability

Stability Performance of Load and No-Load Funds during Declining Market Period of 1962

Between December 31, 1961, and June 28, 1962, mutual funds *on the average* declined 21.5%, adjusted for distributions. Only three mutual funds gained in asset value per share. They were load funds of the "bond" or "bond/preferred stock" variety. Apparently, their good showing may be attributed to management performance. Of the most stable funds in the 1962 market decline seven were no-loads, while 25 were loads. Of the poorest performing 25 funds, one was a no-load and 24 were loads.

Stability Performance of Load and No-Load Funds during Declining Market Period of 1966

Between the high of February 9, 1966, and the low of October 7, 1966, mutual funds *on the average* declined 19.6%, adjusted for distributions. Out of 233 mutual funds, performance ranged from one fund that gained 3.9% to another fund that dropped 36.6%. Both were load funds. Twenty-one no-load funds (about 66% of the total of 33 no-load funds in the tabulation), demonstrated above average resistance to the 1966 decline. One hundred and one load funds (about 50% of the total of 200 load funds in the tabulation) had above average resistance to the decline. About 33% of the no-loads and 50% of the loads performed below average.

Of the 25 best performing funds in 1966 (including 4 no-loads), 18 were bond funds, preferred stock funds, balanced funds, or income funds with a defensive investment policy that stressed investments in bonds and preferred stocks. Of the 25 poorest performing funds in 1966 (including 3 no-loads), *all* were growth funds, specialized funds, and common stock funds.

The stability figures again confirm the Wharton Report's conclusion (echoed by *FundScope*) that performance—in this case price stability performance—has no correlation with the presence or absence of a sales charge. The figures also suggest that if you seek price stability of your investment, your primary consideration should not be the acquisition cost but the type of fund, its investment policy, its portfolio composition, and management competence as reflected in performance results.

Income

Comparing no-load and load fund performances in growth or stability may still not help you if your investment objective is *income*. If you are retired, close to retirement, or desire income, the comparative performance of loads and no-loads could be of keen interest to you. Because of the shorter period of time remaining during which the sales charge can be made up by an increase in the value of your investment, this factor should be seriously considered. If you are retired or close to the usual retirement age of 65, and you invest $10,000 in a load fund, $9,150 will usually be invested. Before your investment shows any profit, $850 must be earned by your share holdings.

One-Year Income Performance Comparisons Between Load and No-Load Funds (1967)

A one-year period is very questionable to use unless you understand that dividends vary widely from year to year. You should never interpret one-year results as indicative of a future yield or a representative yield from a fund. You should also remember that income is computed *not* on asset value but on *offering price*.

Of the top-performing 25 funds, the 1967 income yield as of September 30, 1967, ranged from 5.87% to 3.50%. One of the 25 was a no-load fund. The top yielding fund at 5.87% was a load fund with a sales charge of 8.3%. Among those funds with the highest yield were funds with the highest sales charges (from 8½% to 8¾%). Among the 25 funds with the lowest income yield, two were no-load funds. Of the 36 no-load funds surveyed, 15 performed above average and 21 below average.

5-Year Income Performance Comparisons Between Load and No-Load Funds (1962–1966)

From January, 1962, through December, 1966, the best-performing fund paid $3,195 in cash dividends, based on an initial investment of $10,000. It was a load fund. The poorest-performing fund paid nothing in cash dividends. It was also a load fund. One no-load fund was among the top 25 performers and two no-loads were among the bottom 25 performers. Of the load funds, 16 were among the top 25 performers and 22 were among the bottom 25 performers. In between, load and no-load funds were scattered indiscriminately with as much disparity in the results among the no-loads as in the results among the loads.

10-Year Income Performance Comparisons Between Load and No-Load Funds (1957–1966)

Based on an assumed investment of $10,000 on January 1, 1957, to December 31, 1966, of the top-performing 25 funds in dividends paid, two were no-loads and fifteen were load funds with sales charges of 8% or higher. Of fifteen no-load funds in existence ten years or longer, eleven were above average and four were below average. *FundScope's* conclusion is inescapable: some no-load funds are among the best performers and some are among the worst; some load funds are among the best performers (including those that charge the highest sales commission) and some load funds are among the worst (including those that charge the highest sales commission).

C. The *Forbes'* Ratings

One more study is revealing. *Forbes* does not compare no-load and load fund performance as such, but from its annual ratings of all funds, conclusions can be drawn about the comparative performance of load and no-load funds by examining the relevant figures carefully. *Forbes* believes that short-term performance of a mutual fund is a very poor criterion of its quality as an investment. Therefore, in its annual August report on mutual funds the magazine rates only consistency of performance in four rising market periods and in four declining market periods. It does not rank funds against each other. (For details on *Forbes'* ratings, see page 61.)

Of the 175 open-end mutual funds rated in August, 1968, 150 were load funds (approximately 85% of the total) and 25 were no-load funds (approximately 15% of the total). Here are the results, with conversions to percentages by the author.

RATINGS	Performance in UP Markets % of Load Funds	Performance in UP Markets % of No-Load Funds	Performance in DOWN Markets % of Load Funds	Performance in DOWN Markets % of No-Load Funds
A+	9%	8%	4%	4%
A	8%	4%	6%	12%
A−	8%	24%	5%	0%
B+	17%	24%	7%	0%
B	15%	20%	21%	24%
B−	8%	4%	11%	8%
C+	13%	8%	15%	24%
C	5%	0%	12%	12%
C−	8%	0%	14%	4%
D+	6%	4%	4%	12%
D	3%	4%	1%	0%

The no-load funds had a small edge in the rising market periods because of the larger percentage of growth funds among them; the load funds did somewhat better in the declining market periods because of the greater number of balanced funds among them and because of a generally better cash flow. The comparative results are unusually close. Once again, there seems to be no correlation between performance and the presence or absence of a sales charge. You should choose a fund in terms of its type, investment objectives, investment policies, management's skills, and long-term results. If these elements are approximately equal, only then will the lowest sales commission or the absence of a sales commision be a significant factor in your investment.

A Shortsighted Criticism of No-Load Funds

There are investors who will judge a fund not only by its performance results but also (and correctly) by additional criteria like the management fee, the ratio of expenses to net assets, the ratio of expenses to net profits, the rate of portfolio turnover, etc. Such investors are frequently among the critics of no-load funds. They contend that there may be hidden costs in a no-load fund which offset the reduced sales commission.

Such critics must, in all fairness, acknowledge that no-load funds tend to be much smaller than load funds because the absence of salesmen tends to limit a fund's asset growth and cash flow. Since size tends to reduce operating expense ratios, the no-load funds generally are at a *disadvantage* from the point of view of operating expenses. On the eve of 1967 the largest load fund had assets near $3 billion, 8 load funds had assets in excess of $1 billion, and 39 load funds had assets in excess of $200 million.

On the other hand, the largest no-load fund (assets were $247 million) was only 1/12th the size of the largest load fund. There were two no-load funds with assets about $200 million. Except for these two and five others, all the no-load funds had assets under

$100 million and seventeen of these had about $10 million or less in assets.

What does all this mean? It means that you cannot expect the average no-load fund to have a low expense ratio. The 1964 median expense of mutual funds was $.72 per $100 of net assets. It was 23.1% of net income. It will be generally higher for a no-load fund at any time as compared with the load funds.

One more point needs emphasizing. A high expense ratio is *not* necessarily significant in a growth fund. But a *low* expense ratio is important if you want income from a fund. A fund pays expenses out of its investment income; what remains goes to shareholders as income dividends. Consequently, *the lower a fund's operating expense, the more it can pay out in dividends to a shareholder*. So, if you want income, the no-load funds generally may disappoint you.

Additional Reasons for the Growing Popularity of No-Load Funds

The growth in the popularity of no-load funds is not all accounted for by inexperienced investors rushing into them with false premises (pages 108–109). The increasing appeal of no-load funds also comes from something new that is happening in mutual funds.

Mutual funds have always been primarily long-term investments. They are not intended to be short-term speculations or in-and-out trades like regular stocks. Recently, some fund managers have begun emphasizing short-term performance. The amazing showing of some funds has generated speculative fever among investors who are pouring millions of dollars into funds that emphasize immediate performance. Some of these performance funds are no-loads. They are among the "go-go" funds discussed in the next chapter.

Three additional reasons can be suggested for the growth of no-loads:

1. No-load funds are growing because more investors are apparently willing to "do-it-themselves." Paying no sales charge and knowing that their investment will not first have to increase by 8.5% in value to make up a sales charge before realizing a gain in net asset value per share, these investors are willing to take the time and the energy to watch their investment, evaluate it, and modify it. They are willing to forego the services of a broker.

2. No-load funds are growing because they advertise more frequently than load funds. While the load funds have brokers to push sales, word-of-mouth and printed advertisements are the chief ways in which no-loads can attract buyers. While mutual fund advertisements must be limited to a fund's name and its purpose, the additional identification as "no-load" and "no sales charge" is catching the eye and interest of more and more investors.

3. Some no-load funds are growing rapidly because they are considered by some to be for short-term gain. The no-load fund is often erroneously thought of as superior for speculation because the sales charges of load funds absorb profits or increase losses if they are frequently bought and sold for short-term gain. It is also true that some no-load funds charge a redemption fee, so that an investor in no-loads ought to consider the expense of frequent redemptions.

While the "go-go" funds are not exclusively no-loads, a growing number of investors find the combination of a no-load fund and its possible emphasis on short-term performance an almost irresistible combination. Many financial experts believe that such an attitude will prove to be perilous. To the performance fund, whether no-load or load, we now turn.

10 The "Go-Go" Funds

A new philosophy has invaded mutual funds. The old, tried-and-true philosophy caters to the patient investor, the cautious person who wants real protection against inflation. It gives him a reasonably safe investment with steady growth, or a reliable yield and basic stability. The new philosophy beckons to the speculative investor, the impatient soul who wants quick returns from a fund that takes high risks.

The clarion call is "Perform!" It demands a meteoric rise in net asset value per share, luscious capital gains, and action—plenty of action! As *Forbes* so aptly put it in the fall of 1968,

> ". . . performance is now the name of the game and the mutual funds are playing it with a will. The performance idea is not universally accepted, of course. But it is widespread enough to have enabled the performance funds to take over 70% of the new sales in the fund market vs. 30% ten years ago."

If you plan to "go-go" with a performance fund, you ought to take a closer look at what it really is instead of settling for its glamour or its promise based on short-term success. I am not ringing an alarm bell. I am sounding an alert.

121

The Ambiguity of the Term "Performance Fund"

What is a "performance fund?" Here is a definition by the vice president of a fund that is commonly considered to be one. He was speaking to an audience at the University of Pennsylvania Law School, which held a two-day conference on mutual funds early in 1967.

". . . the term performance fund has been incorrectly used to categorize a small group of capital appreciation funds whose recent gains in per share value have attracted widespread investor notice and new investor money.

"I suggest to you that the term performance fund as presently used is a misnomer and needs clarification. In my opinion, a performance fund is any fund which achieves its stated objective, and in competition with funds which have truly comparable objectives and policies, achieves relatively superior results over a reasonable period of time."

This definition is no help. Every fund *wants* to perform well. Every fund *strives* to perform well. Many funds *do* perform well. According to the speaker, *any* successful fund is a "performance fund." Why, then, do thousands of brokers, investors, Wall Street observers, and financial experts insist on using the term "go-go" to describe a particular kind of fund which is so conspicuous and so alluring?

A Performance Fund Manager Describes His Fund

Introducing the methods and policies used by his fund, the performance fund vice president quoted above went on to pinpoint three elements of successful fund management: first, the management personnel; second, the portfolio policies; third, the investment philosophy of the management. So far, every mutual fund manager in the country would agree with him!

Let us take a closer look at what he had to say about each of these three factors to see whether we can find some distinguishing features of his fund that have earned it the title of "performance fund" or "go-go" fund. Since such funds constitute a *minority* of all American mutual funds, some of his statements will probably represent a *minority view* of mutual fund management philosophy, providing us with clues to some of the unique features of a "go-go" fund. We will quote his remarks on the three aspects of the fund he managed and comment on each.

I. MANAGEMENT PERSONNEL

"A contemporary mutual fund organization depends upon management and communications. Management is the heart and the soul of an organization. It is imperative that only the most competent minds be hired for analytical and portfolio management work. There is no substitute for investment talent. These money managers must understand the goal and be properly motivated to obtain it. Since money management is a highly individualistic art, an atmosphere conducive to creativity and individualism must be established. In conjunction with this, management must be effectively compensated, with significant monetary rewards, but more importantly, with freedom, authority and responsibility. It should be noted that management can reach optimum effectiveness only when equipped with the best tools available. This includes an up-to-date knowledge of the most contemporary methods of both fundamental and technical analysis.

"There is a Spanish saying: 'What the fool does in the end, the wise man does in the beginning.' Timing in today's dynamic investment arena is vital, and so we must concern ourselves with the process of communication within an organization. Information must be gathered, sifted, and evaluated immediately.

"Particular priority must be given to processing negative information. Time delays in evaluating such information can be extremely costly. Sources of information must be continually checked, assessed, and updated. There is a trend toward the creation of total in-house research capability. Such capability reduces the firm's dependence on outside sources and ultimately offers optimum control over investment results. The time required for decision making processes must be constantly reduced. If committees prove cumbersome, they must be replaced. The most effective means must be employed to streamline communication and decision making."

Comments

All fund managers would accept the speaker's opening remarks about the need for management skill. He then emphasizes the individualism, creativity, and freedom that is encouraged by his fund, perhaps more than most funds. On what he says about adequate reward, good tools, good timing, and good communication, all fund managers would also probably agree. But then he strikes a new note, the need for immediacy, for rapid *action,* for locating negative as well as positive market information so that delay in decisions is eliminated. This implies that much intense activity must go on *constantly.* Many fund managers would likely reject this hectic pacing of investment decisions, preferring a safer, more patient, watch-and-wait policy. He then emphasizes the need for absolute sovereignty of the fund in its research capability, cutting its reliance on any outside resources so that the fund may achieve a unique self-containment and identity. Many fund managers would probably strive instead to make use of as many outside and available research resources as possible. Finally, he reiterates the need for speed in decision making and the swift reshuffling of slow-moving personnel groups. Such rapidity in decisions and such innovative personnel policies would probably be avoided by many fund managers.

I. PORTFOLIO POLICIES
"The second element of successful fund management relates to the actual portfolio policies practiced by the firm. The variance in

policy views is considerable but the policies at (name of fund) are as follows:

"First, relative concentration. This results in a sharper focus on companies of particular interest. A policy of selectivity leads to greater control over the portfolio, and, among other things, helps to avoid overstaying in a deteriorating situation.

"Second, relative marketability. A fund must be able to establish and eliminate positions in the shortest possible time period with the least impact on the price of the stock. This fund has always had an interest in the Most Active (Stock) List which usually gives a day-to-day closeup of current trends. When placed in the proper perspective, this can be very revealing.

"Third, relative quality. If you can achieve superior performance with well-timed decisions in quality securities, you will have achieved the qualitative performance referred to earlier. This is the ultimate mark of professionalism to which many fund managers aspire and which very few of them attain.

"Fourth, relative activity. We live in a world where change is the one certainty, a world where there is a running historical struggle between the comforts of the status quo and the continuous pressure for change. It is absolutely imperative the management be sensitive to change . . . In so far as activity reflects this sensitivity for the serious and well-considered efforts of management to attain its objectives for its shareholders, we regard such activity not only as acceptable but as an integral part of our obligation.

"Perhaps the words of T. H. Huxley best express the attitude of (name of fund) management group toward activity: 'The great end of life is not knowledge, but action.' "

Comments

All funds have a relative portfolio concentration among common stocks, preferred stocks, bonds, etc.; so the major clue must lie in the phrase "sharper focus on companies of particular interest." What kind of companies does he mean? While he does not say, they will presumably be unusual companies: they may be little-known but very promising in a rapidly expanding industry, having undergone major management or product changes. They may be highly innovative in personnel policies and business procedures. They may be small but pioneering companies, or they may be firms that have shown spectacular profits. A performance fund management will seize on shares in such companies, while a more conservative fund management will wait and see.

The speaker moves on to the need for rapid and frequent portfolio turnover guided by a daily knowledge of market trends. The average mutual fund portfolio turnover in 1966 was 29.9%. Compare that with the 50%, 75%, 100% turnover of some performance funds today and you get some idea of what the speaker means. It takes boldness, courage, and nerve to buy and sell in one year half or more of the securities in a fund's portfolio. In his remarks on relative quality of portfolio, the speaker again says timing is of the essence, implying speed and frequency in buying and selling.

Finally, taking a cue from the physical scientist, he makes an eloquent plea for *adaptability* to our changing world through a willingness to act quickly. The world demands that each of us "go, go, go." Extending that philosophy to his fund, he insists that the less active it is in seeking shareholder profits, the further it is from the facts of life.

III. PHILOSOPHY OF MANAGEMENT

"Of paramount importance is the concept of flexibility. The sensitivity to change mentioned earlier is the cornerstone to successful investing. Of equal importance to the performance-oriented investor is a profound belief in innovation. Management must demonstrate the willingness to try the untried, and must continuously develop the most contemporary methods and procedures to do the job.

"Something that is very helpful to our group is the recognition that ours is a fallible art. Realistically, we must be prepared to make mistakes, to profit from them, and then to forget them. I believe it is safe to say that all performance funds have an understood philosophy of industriousness. Performance can be equated with hard work. Lastly, we have a fundamental belief in the individual and in the continuity of management. Our policy, reduced to its simplest terms, can be stated in this way: Hire men more intelligent than you are, and then people more intelligent than they."

Comment

While top management in some American businesses stresses the human need for creativity, the *degree* of its willingness to innovate in techniques ranges from the most backward to the most progressive. The speaker's fund might be put close to the far edge of the progressive end. Its capacity for self-criticism and its eagerness to profit from inevitable mistakes—optimistically anticipated—is boldly asserted. Its continuous search for intelligent managers, and then even more intelligent managers, strikes a dynamic note.

Summary Comment

In these remarks the emphases have been unmistakable. The speaker stresses individualism and creativity in management, urgency and swiftness in investment decisions, independence in research, and quick changes of ineffective personnel. He urges streamlining communication, a strong focus on promising, unusual companies, and quick timing in buying and selling securities. He calls for constant innovations in management and investment methods, the capacity for self-criticism, a readiness to adapt quickly to market changes, and emphasis on employee intelligence and quick-wittedness rather than on seniority. These policies are placed in bold relief when you consider that most mutual funds are relatively old-fashioned in their management techniques.

The "Go-Go" Pattern of Performance

The fund managed by the speaker that I have been quoting increased 61% in net asset value per share between October, 1965, and August, 1968. How did *similar* funds perform in the past few years? In 1967, one no-load fund increased an almost unbelievable 301% in net asset value per share! Another, a load fund, went up 116%; 25 others went up at least 50% or more; five of them went up between 25% and 50%.

By September, 1968, 21 performance funds had gone up from between 4% to 113%. Smack in the middle of the uncertain 1968 summer market, one of the best-known mutual fund management companies sent its shareholders a three-page leaflet announcing the inauguration of a *special* fund. We quote from the remarks of the chairman of this fund, announcing the birth:

> "Your Fund was organized on August 8, 1967, as a private investment company. On December 29, 1967, the Fund filed a Registration Statement and Prospectus with the Securities and Exchange Commission so that its shares could be offered to the public. On April 22, 1968, the initial public offering commenced.
>
> "Market acceptance of the Special Fund has indeed been gratifying. When the initial offering began, the Fund was approximately $1,500,000 in size with less than 140,000 shares outstanding. *A little more than two months later, on June 30, the Fund had increased in size to $14,520,057 with over 940,000 shares outstanding.*" (Italics mine.)

The Chairman of this Special Fund likened its policies and portfolio to the four points of a compass, summed up under N.E.W.S. as follows:

N.E.W.S.

"NEW companies—those which are developing new products, new processes, and/or new services. In large measure these companies will be small in size. Their earnings prospects will have to be dramatic for the Fund to invest in them.

"ENERGIZED companies—those whose profit potential has not been fully realized and which have acquired a new management 'team' to turn them around. By new management we don't mean just a vice-president or a new chief executive officer, but a new top management plus a mandate from the Board of Directors to implement constructive changes in policy.

"WORKOUT situations—those companies which have fallen into decay, due largely to management or lack of management, which are attracting outside interest in sufficient size as to create either a favorable merger or tender offer possibilities. These prospects would have to appear to be of near-term nature for the Fund to take aggressive interest.

"SEASONED companies—those which through a significant product or service innovation, or a change in demand for existing product or service innovation, are in a position to enjoy a period of significantly higher profitability.

"Your Fund will generally own all four types of securities. However, the weighting of each category will vary, from time to time, as we move in quest of better opportunities."

Note what the chairman of the newly established performance fund had to say about its portfolio:

"As of June 30 your Fund was 72% invested in equities. We anticipate that this figure may fluctuate rather widely from time to time, depending on the flow of new funds and the availability of appropriate investment opportunities. It should also be noted that the Fund's holdings will be fairly concentrated. Presently the Fund owns 35 issues. While concentration may add risk to the Fund, in contrast to broader diversification, it means that you are really getting what in our judgment are the top selections of favorably changing situations."

How did this newborn fund do in its early days?

"On April 22, 1968, when the public offering began, the value of each of your Fund's shares stood at $12.95. By the end of April this figure had reached $13.35; on May 31, it was $13.99; and on June 30 your Fund's per share value was $14.27. Over these 70 days each share of your Fund increased 10.2%."

This is one sample of what was happening in 1968. Throughout the year (irrespective of urban strife, the Vietnam war, the presidential election, or market slumps), this is the type of fund that was frequently born. It was swamped with money from investors.

Furthermore, newness or size had nothing to do with the results of performance funds in 1968. A family of three funds, with assets over $3 billion, did well; so did another fund with $2.5 billion and a third fund with $600 million. On the other hand, one fund, with only $600,000 in assets in April, 1968, jumped 72% in its asset value per share by August 19th and had to suspend acceptance of new purchase orders because it had grown to $12 million in assets (almost 24 times its original size!) and could not keep up with the influx of orders. Example after example could be cited. For load funds in general, of the 150 funds rated by *Forbes* in August, 1968, 108 (or 72%) outperformed the market; of the 25 no-loads, 16 (or 64%) outperformed the market.

The Cult of Performance

Most mutual funds had a good year in 1967; the broad market trend was up. In such a market, a fund favoring glamour stocks and rapid speculation is bound to thrive. When the market declined briefly in 1968, these funds usually showed decreases in asset value; yet, investors' money poured into performance funds. Furthermore, many performance funds came into existence in response to popular demand. True, the market rallied in April, following President Johnson's announcement about de-escalation in Vietnam and his decision not to run for re-election. But then it dropped in July and August. In September, the market rallied again, and closed generally higher at the end of the year.

The point is that despite market ups and downs, domestic crises, and foreign affairs complications, millions of investors in 1968 went marching on and on, right into performance funds, in fair weather and foul. But despite the striking performance pattern of some "go-go" funds and the pervasive optimism which seems to reign among investors buying into them, some words of caution are in order if you are planning to join the crowd.

The Realities of "Go-Go" Funds

Your investment goals are *your* decision. If you are inclined toward a "go-go" fund, you ought to go into it with your eyes wide open and adjust your goal to the realities of such a fund. It will be sheer folly to invest in a fund whose character and nature are in conflict with your purposes. What are the realities of the "go-go" fund, based on the evidence?

First, "go-go" funds are not necessarily the best for long-term investing. I made twelve telephone calls to as many brokers and asked this question: "If you could sum up in one sentence for a prospective mutual fund investor the single most important idea that he ought to grasp about a 'go-go' fund, what would it be?" The response was unanimous: boiled down, it said, "He ought to know the difference between 'top performance' and 'consistency of performance.' " None of the brokers was hostile to performance funds (most of them are load funds), but the note of caution was unmistakable and the confusion they found among investors was widespread.

"Top performance" by any investment cannot last because of the tie-in between particular securities and the entire securities market. There must be steep declines, slow declines, plateaus, slow rises and sharp rises. In addition, the history of the securities market repeatedly illustrates the truth that what is "top" today may be "bottom" tomorrow. In contrast, "consistency of performance" is, by its very definition, that which *does last*. It can be achieved and it has been achieved by many funds. If you want a mutual fund for long-term investment, for 5, 10, 15, or 20 years, then it is consistency that you should emphasize and it is patience that you must exercise.

Second, a "go-go" fund's pursuit of short-term gains is legally limited. Mutual fund managers, dealers, and brokers generally agree that funds are not for short-term speculation. If you want to use funds that way, remember the law which says that if 30% of a fund's income comes from profits in stocks held less than 90 days, then the fund loses its "conduit" privilege and pays regular corporate taxes on all its income rather than being able to pass its income on to the shareholders. That means that even a performance fund cannot immediately pay you profits after a good trading period but must retain, for the 90-day period, at least 70% of all its income. Stated another way, 90 days is a much longer period to wait for a profit than you may wish. But, legally, all funds *must* wait if they want "conduit" privileges. In that 90-day period, much can happen.

Third, speculation with go-go funds may be expensive. If you want to turn a quick profit by getting into performance funds when they are low and out when they are high, the sales commission on frequent buying and possible redemption fees for selling will both mount. Furthermore, if you sell your shares in a go-go fund before six months have elapsed since your purchase, you cannot claim the "long-term capital gain" exemption. Adding up the sales commissions, the redemption fees, and the loss of long-term capital gain tax allowance may increase your expenses. They may either equal or exceed a substantial part of the gain in your investment. Finally, you will find it difficult to convince a reputable broker that he should help you in such "churning"—he will likely lose his securities license if he does!

The performance fever spawns geniuses who want to start a fund. The vice-president of one fund is quoted by *Forbes* as saying, "I get several calls a day from people wanting to start mutual funds. They're coming out of the woodwork and very few have any idea what they're doing." But the genius invests money, has temporary success, and attracts more money to invest. He may buy speculative stocks which go up; his performance is duly noted and brokers bring him more customers and more money. It continues, in a soaring spiral, but what is the fund actually built on? Many investment experts would seriously question whether this is really a mutual fund.

If, after considering these points carefully, you are sure of what you want, willing to assume risks and willing to endure loss as well as anticipate gain, you may be quite happy in a go-go fund. From sources listed in Appendix I you can locate the names of most of the prominent go-go funds. They are appearing rapidly. Any list of them is usually obsolete within a week. If it is a go-go fund that you want, you owe it to yourself to learn all that you possibly can about it.

The future of these performance funds is a big question mark. It all depends on the interplay of several factors: the United States economy, market conditions, and the attitude of investors.

11　Mutual Fund Investment Plans

You can easily become swamped with mutual fund sales brochures, pamphlets, charts, booklets, and statistical tables which try to help you determine your future financial needs. These materials dramatize the money problems that you may face in the future, problems like limited social security and pension income, the effect of inflation on your savings, educational expenses for your children, and unforeseen emergencies. Chances are you do not have to be "sold" on these problems because you are acutely aware of them already from observing others and from your own personal experiences. Among younger people, the competition for jobs, the high cost of living, and the many uncertainties of the future make them well aware of the many contingencies that they will face.

What you probably seek is clear, down-to-earth help in making investment plans. You want realism rather than clichés, candid details instead of grandiose projections. Any good, long-term mutual fund investment is one of the best ways to prepare for whatever financial demands the future will make on you. The psychological security from a good investment is probably far more important than your being able to pinpoint exactly how you will use the investment in the future.

Recapitulation of Salient Facts about Mutual Fund Investments

If you have read each chapter in this book, you will have met certain recurrent ideas. Experienced brokers and investment counselors affirm that those ideas cannot be repeated too often and that they ought constantly to be remembered before and after you invest in mutual funds. They are reviewed here:

—No rate of return on a mutual fund investment can be guaranteed.

—Mutual funds are long-term investments, usually affording neither spectacular results nor quick profits.

—Mutual funds are not for trading.

—The main purposes of most mutual funds are growth, income or price stability.

—Before you consider investing in mutual funds, you ought to have an adequate savings account for emergencies as well as an adequate life insurance program.

—Mutual fund shares can be liquidated any time you desire.

—Investigate before you invest, and review your investment periodically.

—As a mutual fund shareholder, you will enjoy many legal protections.

—There is no relationship between the sales charge (or lack of one) and the performance of a fund.

—Performance funds ("go-go" funds) are generally the most speculative, offering opportunities for greater gain as well as opportunities for greater losses.

When Should You Invest in Mutual Funds?

Most equity investments pose perennial problems: what to buy, when to buy, how long to hold, when to sell, and how much to sell. Were you faced with such questions, you might be bombarded by all kinds of friendly and conflicting advice by self-styled "masters of the market." Investing in mutual funds eliminates a number of these imponderables. Furthermore, risk is minimized through portfolio diversification. Simply stated, the time to buy mutual funds is when you have the money and when you can afford to.

If you invest regularly, you will receive the benefits of "dollar-cost averaging." Dollar-cost averaging is simply *systematic* investing. It is a formula which demonstrates, mathematically, that any time is a good time to invest in a mutual fund provided that you invest regularly thereafter. You cannot pick the top or the bottom of the market but if you will invest the same dollar amount at regular intervals, whether the price is moving up or down, you will reap the benefits of the lowest average cost per share. Any time, then, is a good time to invest in mutual funds as long as you follow through with regular, periodic investments in an amount that you can afford.

Sophisticated mutual fund investors go even further. They invest in several funds with similar investment objectives. They then research the price activity history of each fund to determine the lowest and the highest net asset values. By closely watching the price fluctuations of each fund in their package, they invest each month in the fund which is selling nearest its lowest average. This could give a better dollar-cost averaging result, and it also hedges against drastic loss in your dollar values during market declines.

Types of Investment Plans

Many funds have a systematic investment program with no minimum initial investment and no minimum periodic investment. Others have initial minimums that range from $10 to $10,000, and periodic minimums from $10 to $500. These minimums may vary from state to state and from time to time. Be sure to check the prospectus carefully to determine current requirements. Systematic investment plans are of two kinds: contractuals and voluntary. Not all funds have both types available.

Contractual Plan. Under this plan you formally agree to make regular, periodic investments for a specified period of time, say $100 a month for ten years. A relatively large percentage of the sales charge for the contractual period is deducted from the investments that you make during the first year (up to 50%). If you terminate the plan before the stipulated period, you lose the amount deducted for the sales charges. Fund companies today are under pressure from the government to modify or to terminate this plan.

Voluntary Plan. Under this plan you can make regular or irregular investments, of similar or varying amounts, but the order that you sign is *not* contractual. It often states, however, what you expect to invest. Most funds, under either voluntary or contractual plans, will automatically reinvest net income and capital gains distributions to purchase additional shares for you unless you request income dividends in cash or the capital gains distributions in cash.

The success of either type of plan depends, in part, on your regular payments. Do not be dismayed by declines in the market. To liquidate *then* would result in a loss; however, to *buy* then would result in your acquiring more shares at a lower average price.

How Much Should You Invest?

Depending on the fund's minimum requirements, you must determine what you can afford to invest. How much others invest should be of no concern to you. Select an amount that *you* can comfortably afford and then invest regularly. After you start your plan, stick with it! Do not abandon it! Abiding by a plan is the best test of a serious investor. Mutual funds are not for haphazard, erratic, or inconsistent investing.

Comparisons of Accumulation Plan Results

In its September, 1968, issue, *FundScope* published a study of the results of accumulation plan investments for all 10, 15, and 20-year periods within the last quarter century.* The magazine used as many funds as were qualified during each period. On the next few pages you will find the tabulated analyses. The figures presented show how long-term investments in mutual funds performed in the past. They are *not* an indication or projection of future performance.

ALL THE DATA ARE BASED ON AN INITIAL INVESTMENT OF $500, WITH $100 MONTHLY INVESTMENTS THEREAFTER. ALL DISTRIBUTIONS FROM CAPITAL GAINS AND DIVIDEND INCOME WERE REINVESTED. NO ADJUSTMENT HAS BEEN MADE FOR INCOME TAXES PAYABLE, BUT ALL COSTS (INCLUDING SALES CHARGE AND REDEMPTION FEE, IF ANY) HAVE BEEN DEDUCTED.

10-Year Periods
Ranked In Descending Order
Average Mutual Fund Results

* All data from *FundScope,* by permission.

Of A Systematic Investment
Program, Total Payments $12,400
($500 Initial, $100 Monthly)
All Distributions Reinvested

The 1968 ten-year data covers 125 mutual funds, as compared to 110 in 1967, 108 in 1966, 95 in 1965, and 65 in 1964. The best of all 10-year periods in the past quarter century ($26,354) was 1947–1956; the worst ($18,420) was 1957–1966.

10-Year Period	Liquidating Value
1947–1956	$26,354
1946–1955	26,229
1949–1958	25,945
1950–1959	24,779
1945–1954	24,593
1952–1961	24,366
1951–1960	22,604
1958–1967	22,092
1943–1952	21,511
1948–1957	20,894
1956–1965	20,753
1954–1963	19,802
1955–1964	19,668
1953–1962	19,291
1944–1953	19,201
1957–1966	18,420

15-Year Periods
Ranked In Descending Order
Average Mutual Fund Results
Of A Systematic Investment
Program, Total Payments $18,400
($500 Initial, $100 Monthly)
All Distributions Reinvested

The 1968 fifteen-year data cover 94 funds, as compared to 85 in 1967, 84 in 1966, 76 in 1965, and 49 in 1964. The best of all 15-year periods ($53,721) was 1947–1961; the worst ($38,808) was 1952–1966.

15-Year Period	Liquidating Value
1947–1961	$53,721
1944–1958	51,807
1945–1959	51,256
1946–1960	46,899
1951–1965	45,974
1949–1963	45,056
1950–1964	44,092
1953–1967	43,624
1948–1962	42,717
1943–1957	41,852
1952–1966	38,808

20-Year Periods
Ranked in Descending Order
Average Mutual Fund Results
Of A Systematic Investment
Program, Total Payments $24,000
($500 Initial, $100 Monthly)
All Distributions Reinvested

The 1968 data cover 51 funds, as compared to 48 in 1967, 46 in 1966, 41 in 1965, and 32 in 1964. The best of all 20-year periods ($84,721) was 1946–1965; the worst ($74,440) was 1947–1966.

20-Year Period	Liquidating Value
1946–1965	$84,721
1948–1967	83,377
1945–1964	81,992
1944–1963	81,305
1943–1962	78,647
1947–1966	74,440

Comments

These comparisons show the advantages of investing in mutual funds in long-term rising markets. Just the opposite would be true in continuously declining markets. The comparisons should also be viewed solely in terms of a particular fund's goals and investment policies. Remember, also, that these are *growth* figures and not income and stability figures. When comparing individual funds, keep in mind that if a fund's main purpose is income rather than growth, or stability rather than growth, then below average growth performance is not necessarily a black mark against the fund.

In each of the periods the performance of individual mutual funds deviated greatly from the average. In the best 20-year period (1946–1965) the average liquidating value was $84,721. Results for individual funds ranged from a high of $147,418 for a growth fund to a low of $31,165 for a bond fund.

FundScope's conclusions are well worth noting:

"1) No one knows which period will prove to be the best or the worst period over a span of many years.

"2) Though some periods will be much better than others, any time is a good time to invest in American industry for the long term.

"3) Careful selection of individual funds is important if you seek average or better-than-average results.

"4) To assure that some purchases will be made at important market bottoms and not just at market tops, at least part of your total mutual fund investments should be spread systematically over a period of years long enough to include one or more major market declines. This method of investing is called 'Dollar-Cost Averaging' . . ."

Lump Sum or Quantity Purchase Plan

Some fortunate investors are able to make a lump-sum investment of anywhere from $2,000 to $100,000. Most funds have reduced sales charges when quantity purchases above $25,000 are
made. The discount schedule is shown in the prospectus. The purchase need not be a single lump-sum purchase to qualify for the
reduced sales charge. If you sign a letter of intent to purchase the
required dollar amount within a period that does not exceed 13
months, you could qualify for the lower sales charges. To qualify
for a reduced sales charge on a lump-sum purchase or through a
letter of intent, the buyer must be (a) a single individual; (b) a
married individual with children under 21; or (c) a trustee of a
single trust estate. In some states, this prevents investment clubs or
other groups from joining together to purchase mutual fund shares
at reduced sales charges.

The performance of a $10,000 lump-sum investment over past
5, 10, 15, and 20-year periods—stressing growth of investment—
was detailed in Chapter 6. All investment figures therein can be
multiplied or divided accordingly for any lump-sum investment over
$10,000. Chapter 6 also contained data on past income perform-
ance and stability performance of funds for which that information
was available.

Additional Suggestions

1. Plan to review your investments periodically with your
broker or on your own. Over an extended period, a change in your
portfolio of funds may be in order because of changes in your objectives and circumstances.

2. Keep as fully informed as you can about the fund(s) in
which you have invested. Read the quarterly and annual reports

carefully. Note portfolio turnover and the number of shares issued and redeemed.

3. Subscribe to at least one publication that annually rates and/or ranks funds in terms of long range and current performance.

4. If your financial condition permits, seriously consider diversifying your fund holdings among several funds with different goals so as to balance your risks and spread your investment dollars among the greatest possible variety of securities.

5. When the market is in a mild or a strong decline, as it inevitably will be, try to relax. Continue your periodic investments, as do the overwhelming number of mutual fund shareholders.

6. Do not hesitate to communicate with your broker or your fund's management to make any inquiry that you have in mind. Since you are paying for their knowledge and experience, you are entitled to their considered reply.

7. Keep a small reserve to take advantage of market declines. Your dollar-cost averaging will improve if you buy a few extra shares when the market is down.

12 Mutual Fund Withdrawal Plans

Which would you rather have: (1) $10,000 in a bank savings account from which you would get a guaranteed $50 a month until the principal is depleted; (2) $10,000 in a savings and loan association account, earning a slightly higher rate of fixed interest and paying a guaranteed $50 a month until the principal is depleted; (3) $10,000 in a mutual fund from which you can withdraw $50 a month while the principal may appreciate or depreciate in value? Eight years ago, 25,000 people chose mutual fund withdrawal plans. By 1968 that number had increased to 200,000. The asset value of their investments was over $4 billion and their checks totalled an estimated average of over $52 million a month.

A mutual fund withdrawal plan is not a goose that lays an infinite number of golden eggs. When market conditions are unfavorable, the goose may develop a lean and hungry look. If economic conditions are favorable, the goose may become very productive. Buying a goose is a risk but it also provides an opportunity for the accumulation of nest eggs.

Notes of Caution

A mutual fund withdrawal plan is not guaranteed. An insurance annuity guarantees you a uniform lifetime income. In return, you have no control of the principal. A mutual fund withdrawal plan does not guarantee you a lifetime income, but you *do* have control of the principal at all times. You may draw on any or all of it, as you wish, and vary the rate of withdrawal. You are not limited to any fixed, preconceived formula in a mutual fund withdrawal plan. In banks or savings and loan associations, your savings earn fixed rates of interest. The principal is also fixed unless you add to it or draw from it. If you draw from it, the principal cannot replenish itself. In a mutual fund withdrawal plan, both the principal and the income can increase or decrease. Again, the risk is greater but so is the opportunity.

Mutual fund withdrawal plans have not been tested in any protracted market decline period. The stock market has steadily risen in the last 8 years except in 1962, 1966 and, briefly, in 1968. When you examine withdrawal plan results in funds that interest you, remember that those results were established during a generally rising trend in the market. The results in a prolonged declining market could be quite different, especially for growth funds as compared to balanced funds. There is no data available for the effect of a long-term market decline on mutual fund withdrawal plans, mainly because there has been no "long-term" market decline since withdrawal plans were begun.

What Is a Mutual Fund Withdrawal Plan?

A mutual fund withdrawal plan is a means by which you can redeem your shares in a planned, systematic way. The basic requirement is an investment of anywhere from $5,000 to $10,000.

Any plan that you set up can be terminated by you at any time for any reason. The only limitation placed on your withdrawals by some funds is a maximum percentage of the account which you can withdraw periodically.

The greatest single advantage of a withdrawal plan is that the remaining balance of your principal is invested and is working for you under the skilled hands of managers. Under long-term, favorable market conditions, your principal could increase in excess of the amount that you have withdrawn periodically.

Who Uses Withdrawal Plans?

Only the investor who has carefully weighed and evaluated his present financial condition and future needs should consider investing in a withdrawal plan. The most important single fact to remember is this: if the investment income from your principal is insufficient to provide your monthly withdrawal requirements, your principal may have to be used. If securities prices decline, investment income will decline and the principal will decline because withdrawal amounts from the principal will have to be increased to maintain a fixed amount of income. It is for this reason that many people seriously consider a variable withdrawal, based upon a percentage of the account balance or the number of shares owned. Mutual funds periodically advise withdrawal plan shareholders as to the exact status of their accounts.

What Purposes Do Withdrawal Plans Serve?

To help you decide on the type of fund that is best for you and the kind of withdrawal plan that you will want to establish, first examine the various purposes a plan may serve. In the following list, check those statements which identify your purposes:

—supplement present earned income
—supplement retirement income
—meet school or college expenses
—care for dependents
—make rent or mortgage payments after retirement
—pay for travel expenses
—meet unexpected emergency bills after retirement
—meet fixed, periodic bills like insurance premiums
—spend for luxury items

One very valuable additional use of a withdrawal plan is in arranging for the distribution of your estate in case of death. Many people prefer that their heirs receive limited, but regular, periodic sums over a set number of years rather than large, lump sums all at once. In addition, they would like remaining money to be intelligently managed rather than to be in the hands of young or inexperienced individuals. Withdrawal plans assume the continued, diversified investment of principal by competent investment management while designated sums are being paid to your beneficiaries.

Which Kind of Fund Is Best to Use in a Withdrawal Plan?

Among the great variety of funds there is no "best" one for everybody. The best type of fund for you depends on market conditions during the periods of your withdrawal program and your particular purposes and financial condition.

Market Conditions

In steadily rising market periods you might wish to consider a *growth fund* or a *common stock fund*. If withdrawals had to be made from principal, they would be compensated for by an increase in the asset value of your investment. From a study of the 10-year withdrawal record of almost 200 mutual funds (on an assumed initial investment of $10,000) the evidence is strong that funds with a growth objective drew, on the average, the *most* from principal; but at the end of ten years the initial $10,000 investment was often worth from $15,000 to $50,000. In a highly fluctuating market or a market with frequent declines you would likely look to an *income fund*. The evidence from almost 200 funds shows that those with an income purpose withdrew the *least* from principal; but after ten years the average asset value of the principal was lower than the average asset value of growth funds.

Personal Considerations

If you are able and willing to vary the amounts of monthly withdrawals, taking more when the market is rising and less when the market is declining, the type of fund will be less important to you than a reasonable withdrawal strategy. A reasonable withdrawal against principal in a rising market may become unreasonable in a declining market and you will be wise to guard against exhausting your principal. If you must have a steady, fixed monthly withdrawal, then you should pick a fund which emphasizes investment income. Regular dividend income from your investment will be more important to you than possible growth in the size of your investment.

If you are concerned by wide market fluctuations and want to lower the risk of exhausting your capital when the market is down, then a "middle of the road" fund may be best for you. In order to pay you a fixed amount each month, such a fund will draw more from principal than an income fund; it will draw less from principal than a growth fund. Though it may give you less dividend income than an income fund and less capital appreciation than a growth fund, it will, during a price decline, generally deplete the principal less rapidly than an income fund or a growth fund.

Protecting Yourself in a "Package" of Funds

We have seen that varying market conditions have different effects on mutual fund withdrawal plan results. To protect yourself, why not own a "package" of funds, one of which performs well in all types of markets? Another protection that you can provide yourself with is to use monthly checks from mutual funds *only* as a supplement to other kinds of income. The other income should be of the fixed dollar type like social security, an annuity, a pension, a savings and loan account, or rental income. Since the future is, as always, unknown, it would be wise to own both fixed dollar investments and mutual fund shares.

The Flexibility of Methods of Withdrawal

Suppose you began a plan with an initial investment of $10,000 that purchased 1,000 shares of Fund X at $10 a share. The following methods of withdrawal plan operation show the great range of possibilities:

1. The payment of a *fixed percentage* (6% is most commonly recommended) of the total money invested in the fund. This is accomplished by liquidating sufficient shares to equal exactly this fixed percentage. The size of the payments will vary according to the net asset value of your total investment.

2. The payment of a *fixed amount* which is accomplished as above. Decide how much you want and in which periods.

3. The liquidation of a *fixed percentage of the total number of shares* owned, with proceeds paid to you or your heirs.

4. The liquidation of a *fixed number of shares.*

5. The payment of *dividend income* only.

6. The payment of *dividend income* and *capital gains* distributions.

7. The payment of *dividend income* and *capital gains* distributions in combination with 1, 2, or 3 above.

There are other possible combinations and methods, but these indicate the flexibility possible. The plan can be set up on a monthly, quarterly, semi-annual, or annual basis. Payment dates can often be altered and rearranged, depending upon the individual fund and its degree of flexibility. You may possibly want to change the basis of your withdrawals after they have begun by changing the number of shares to be liquidated, the percentage of total capital withdrawn, or any of the other variable factors.

The variety of withdrawal plan options contrasts with the relatively limited options available in annuities or life insurance policies. Also, some fund investors have made "inter-vivos" trust arrangements for ownership of their fund accounts. They make such trusts (or the custodian bank used by their funds) the beneficiary of their life insurance policies. Using this system, the lump-sum death benefit would be immediately invested under the terms of the trust agreement. It may be split up among several different funds, or concentrated in one fund, or invested in a combination of funds, bond, and common stocks. Investors using this "inter-vivos" trust plan seem to feel that their widows and other heirs could realize greater financial gain than if they were to settle for the 2½% or 3% interest rate that would apply if the proceeds of their life insurance were held under one of the options of their life insurance company.

Additional Conveniences of a Withdrawal Plan

In addition to the privilege of changing the basis for your withdrawals, you

(1) may have your checks sent directly to your bank for deposit;

(2) may terminate the plan or suspend payments whenever you wish;

(3) will receive periodic statements of your account indicating current and all previous transactions;

(4) will receive an annual statement for income tax purposes showing amounts paid to you that are taxable as capital gains distributions and dividends.

Taking Precautions

You can protect yourself in a mutual fund withdrawal plan in at least two of the following three ways:

First, if you have sufficient initial capital ($15,000 to $20,000), you should establish withdrawal programs in at least two funds, one a good balanced fund and the other an income fund which has an above average record in declining markets.

Second, if you must limit yourself to one fund, choose a variable type of withdrawal plan which will reduce the risk of exhausting your invested capital. You must be willing to accept a varying amount of withdrawal dollars over the years ahead, depending upon market conditions.

Third, whether you are in one or two funds, periodically re-examine the condition of your plan and be ready to modify it when market conditions justify the change. Calculate the value of the total number of shares left in your account, altering yourself to any change in the asset value per share since your last calculation.

This will help you decide whether to adjust monthly withdrawals on the basis of increasing or decreasing asset value, so that your capital is not depleted. Your total number of shares is vitally important because dividends are paid on that basis. If the number of shares owned remains fairly consistent, then your capital is probably not being greatly reduced. If you see that your share holdings are decreasing, be alert to the possibility of changing your monthly withdrawals to keep as much of your original capital as intact as possible.

Deciding on a Plan

There are two major types of withdrawal plans: the *fixed* amount ("level payment") and the *variable* amount ("variable payment"). Your choice between the two should depend on whether your major requirement is to conserve your initial capital. A level payment plan gives less protection to capital, while a variable payment plan gives more.

If you want to pay off a 5-year loan, send a child through school, travel for several years, or fulfill relatively short-term mortgage payment obligations, then depletion of your capital will not concern you. You can add more to the capital or use the remainder in any way you choose, once your short-term obligations are met.

If depletion of the capital is something that you cannot tolerate, then you would be wise to consider a plan which provides variable dollar withdrawals. If you wish to supplement your social security, annuity, or pension, then it is essential for you to preserve your capital in order to receive sufficient dividends and capital gains distributions.

Different Kinds of Withdrawals in the Variable Plan

The level payment plan is simple to understand and execute. You decide on a fixed sum for periodic withdrawals and that's that. But the variable plan can be carried out in a number of ways, depending on market conditions. You may request your fund to liquidate a minimum number of shares each month. When the net asset value per share is high, you get a bigger check; when it is low, you get a smaller check. By carefully observing the number of shares that you own, you can adjust your withdrawals for short-term periods. There will be little risk of depletion of your capital because of a declining market. There is the possibility that when the net asset value of your shares decreases, your income may become too low for your purposes. That is why, if you select this type of approach, you ought to have other sources of income to supplement your withdrawal check.

If you are fortunate enough to be able to invest in two funds, you could draw a fixed sum from one fund and arrange for the liquidation of a fixed number of shares or percentage of assets from the other fund. Here you are offsetting the capital depletion of your investment in the first fund by "rolling with the punches" in your second fund.

A third possibility is to determine your life expectancy according to Section 1.72–9, Table 1, Federal Income Tax Regulations, and calculate monthly payments accordingly. It would seem to be the better part of wisdom for anyone retiring between 63 and 68 to provide a capital sum that will not be depleted in less than 15 years, or 180 months. *If* stock market prices rise, you can increase the percentage of your withdrawal amounts. If the market declines, hold to the same percentage but expect smaller checks. If that does happen, you could still get varying payments for as long as you live, depending upon the fund.

Withdrawal Amounts

It is impossible to give any recommended figure, though 6% is common. It depends on your wishes and your needs. Remember, always, that if the amount you want exceeds the earned dividend income and the capital gains distributions, your principal may be substantially reduced in a declining market. Most investors determine the monthly withdrawal dollar amount on one of the following bases:

Illustration of Assumed Investment in X Growth Fund

The table below covers the period from January 1, 1958 to December 31, 1967. This was a period during which common stock prices fluctuated, but were generally higher at the end of the period than at the beginning. It is assumed that shares were purchased at the beginning of the period at the cost shown in the table and that at least the minimum amount indicated was withdrawn each month. The results reflect the operation of a withdrawal plan under the terms of which all investment income dividends and capital gains distributions are reinvested in additional shares at net asset value and sufficient shares are sold from the shareowner's account at the time of each withdrawal payment to provide for such payment. Continued withdrawals in excess of current income will eventually exhaust principal, particularly in a period of declining market prices. The results shown should not be considered as a representation of the dividend income, capital gains or losses, or amount available for withdrawal from an investment made in the X Fund today. Only that portion of the total amount withdrawn designated "From Investment Income Dividends" should be regarded as income; the remainder represents a withdrawal of principal.

ILLUSTRATION OF AN ASSUMED INVESTMENT OF $10,000 BASED ON INITIAL
NET ASSET VALUE OF $9,150 WITH $50 WITHDRAWN EACH MONTH

Year Ended 12/31	AMOUNTS WITHDRAWN *				VALUE OF REMAINING SHARES *		
	From Investment Income Dividends†	From Principal	Amount Total	Cumulative Total	Value Of Remaining Original Shares	Value Of Shares Acquired Through Capital Gains Distributions[1] †	Total Value Of Shares Held At Year-End
1958	$240	$360	$600	$ 600	$11,198	$ 675	$11,873
1959	210	390	600	1,200	11,600	1,300	12,900
1960	247	353	600	1,800	10,100	1,650	11,750
1961	180	420	600	2,400	10,970	2,040	13,010
1962	225	375	600	3,000	9,000	1,030	10,030
1963	150	450	600	3,600	9,800	2,010	11,810

1964	138	462	600	4,200	9,300	2,610	11,910
1965	167	433	600	4,800	12,348	3,600	15,948
1966	205	395	600	5,400	11,200	2,910	14,110
1967	183	417	600	6,000	15,230	7,054	22,284
TOTAL	$1,945	$4,045	$6,000				

1 The dollar amounts of capital gains distributions accepted in shares were 1958—$540; 1959—$605; 1960—$458; 1961—$310; 1962—$260; 1963—$90; 1964—$120; 1965—$210; 1966—$655; 1967—$2,100. Total—$5,348.

* The figures in these illustrations are based on the assumption that withdrawals were made first from income for the year, as measured by the investment income dividends reinvested that year, and then from principal, as represented by the original shares acquired.

† No adjustment has been made for any income taxes payable by shareowners on investment income dividends and capital gains distributions or on any net capital gains realized on the liquidation of shares in connection with periodic withdrawals.

1. fixed amounts based on a percentage of their total investment;

2. an amount equal to $\frac{1}{12}$ of the fund's previous year's earned annual income;

3. an amount equal to $\frac{1}{12}$ of the fund's previous year's earned annual dividend and capital gains distributions;

4. an amount equal to $\frac{1}{12}$ of a percentage (3%, 4%, 5%, or 6%) of the account's net asset value at the beginning of each year.

The details on the amount to be withdrawn can be explored and studied with your broker, who can advise you in the light of your particular circumstances.

How to Read Withdrawal Plan Charts

As part of their sales literature, many mutual funds provide illustrations of how you might have fared had you invested in a withdrawal plan with that fund for a 10-year period. The investments represent amounts of $10,000, $25,000, $50,000, or $100,000. If you are considering a withdrawal plan, it will help to familiarize yourself with what one of these charts looks like so that you can understand what you are reading.

The two preceding illustrative charts have only one purpose: to assist you in reading such a chart and to suggest a few guidelines that you can apply in interpreting it. *In no way are these charts intended to represent the actual performance of any particular fund. They do not represent a "good" or a "bad" performance. They in no way represent an "average standard" performance against which you should measure the record of any particular fund. They are in no way offered as "typical" of the performance of the type of fund with which they are identified.*

The charts are simply examples of the format with which funds illustrate their withdrawal plan results. Following each chart, we suggest a few hints which may help you in reading them.

Comments on Withdrawal Program Chart, X Growth Fund

The second, third, seventh, and eighth columns are always the most significant ones for you to study in any record of a withdrawal plan.

Column II: *Amounts Withdrawn From Investment Income Dividends.* To most investors in a growth fund withdrawal program, investment income dividends are of secondary importance. They fully expect the likelihood of the major source of the withdrawals coming from principal, though this is not to suggest that some growth funds do not have high dividend income. In the example given, income dividends accounted for only approximately ⅓ of the investor's withdrawals over ten years ($1,945).

Column III: *Amounts Withdrawn From Principal.* In the above example, withdrawal from principal outstripped withdrawals from dividends by 2 to 1, ($4,045 and $1,945) and constituted ⅔ of the investor's total withdrawals over ten years ($4,045 of $6,000). This, too, is a common pattern in growth funds.

Column VII: *Value Of Shares Acquired Through Capital Gains Distributions.* The value of the reinvested capital gains distributions is what each year kept the total value of the investment higher than it might have been had the capital gains distributions been taken in cash. (The amounts are listed in footnote 1.)

Column VIII: *Total Value of Shares Held At Year-End.* In no year did the total value of shares held at year-end fall below the initial net asset value. In only two years, 1962 and 1966, did the total value at year-end fall below what it had been the previous year. Over the entire life of the investment, the final total value had increased close to 144% (from an initial value of $9,150 to a final value of $22,284).

Let us look now at an example of a withdrawal program performance in an income fund.

Illustration of Assumed Investment in Y Income Fund

The table below covers the period from January 1, 1958 to December 31, 1967. This was a period during which common stock prices fluctuated, but were generally higher at the end of the period than at the beginning. It is assumed that shares were purchased at the beginning of the period at the costs shown in the table and that at least the minimum amount indicated was withdrawn each month. The results reflect the operation of a withdrawal plan under the terms of which all investment income dividends and capital gains distributions are reinvested in additional shares at net asset value and sufficient shares are sold from the shareowner's account at the time of each withdrawal payment to provide for such payment. Continued withdrawals in excess of current income will eventually exhaust principal, particularly in a period of declining market prices. The results shown should not be considered as a representation of the dividend income, capital gains or losses, or amount available for withdrawal from an investment made in the Y Fund today. Only that portion of the total amount withdrawal designated "From Investment Income Dividends" should be regarded as income; the remainder represents a withdrawal of principal.

ILLUSTRATION OF AN ASSUMED INVESTMENT OF $10,000 BASED ON INITIAL NET ASSET VALUE OF $9,150 WITH $50 WITHDRAWN EACH MONTH

Year Ended 12/31	AMOUNTS WITHDRAWN *				VALUE OF REMAINING SHARES *		
	From Investment Income Dividends**	From Principal	Amount Total	Cumulative Total	Value Of Remaining Original Shares	Value Of Shares Acquired Through Capital Gains Distributions[1]**	Total Value Of Shares Held At Year-End
1958	$580	$20	$600	$ 600	$12,380	$ 498	$12,878
1959	553	47	600	1,200	11,410	1,555	12,965
1960	600	—	600	1,800	11,755	2,044	13,799
1961	600	—	600	2,400	12,100	2,940	15,040
1962	600	—	600	3,000	11,701	3,167	14,868
1963	590	10	600	3,600	12,850	3,705	16,555

Year						
1964	560	40	4,200	13,100	4,050	17,150
1965	600	—	4,800	13,842	4,675	18,517
1966	600	—	5,400	12,657	3,879	16,536
1967	600	600	6,000	13,254	4,800	18,054
TOTAL	$5,883	$117	$6,000			

1 The dollar amounts of capital gains distributions accepted in shares were 1958—$410; 1959—$1,154; 1960—$630; 1961—$620; 1962—$308; 1963—$420; 1964—$390; 1965—$410; 1966—$210; 1967—$505. Total—$5,057.

* The figures in these illustrations are based on the assumption that withdrawals were made first from income for the year, as measured by the investment income dividends reinvested that year, and then from principal, as represented by the original shares acquired.

** No adjustment has been made for any income taxes payable by shareholders on investment income dividends and capital gains distributions or on any net capital gains realized on the liquidation of shares in connection with periodic withdrawals.

Comments on Withdrawal Program Chart, Y Income Fund

Column II: *Amounts Withdrawn From Investment Income Dividends*. To investors in an income fund the investment income dividends are of primary importance. The investor expects that the major source of the withdrawals will be from the income dividends and that little, if any, of the principal will be depleted unless the market declines. In the example given, the income dividends were sufficient to account for 97% of the $6,000 in withdrawals over 10 years. In the market decline years of 1962 and 1966 the income dividends held to the 6% withdrawal figure.

Column III: *Amounts Withdrawn From Principal*. In the example, in only four years was the principal depleted and then by very small amounts. Throughout the 10-year period, stability of the original investment was maintained.

Column VII: *Value of Shares Acquired Through Capital Gains Distributions*. The value of the reinvested capital gains distributions kept the total value of the investment higher than it might have been had the capital gains distributions been taken in cash. (The amounts are listed in footnote 1.)

Column VIII: *Total Value of Shares Held At Year-End*. In all years through the investment period the value of the original investment had appreciated, though in 1962 and 1966 the value dropped from what it was in 1961 and 1965. Because of the generally increasing market during the decade, the total value of the investment increased by close to 100% (from an initial value of $9,150 to a final total value of $18,054). So the fund achieved growth as well as maintaining income purposes.

General Comments on Examples of Withdrawal Programs

Clearly, when you read a withdrawal performance chart, you must interpret the figures in terms of the fund's stated goals. When you compare withdrawal performances among funds that you may be considering, be sure that you compare similar types of funds. The introductory remarks preceding the statistical information in each chart are standard requirements by the SEC. The fund must not depict the withdrawal program as representative of future performance. It is also obliged to give a general description of the market conditions within which the program operated. The double-asterisked footnotes are most important. The $6,000 withdrawn over ten years is not "in-the-pocket." Part of it would have to be paid in income taxes, the amount depending on your tax bracket. It is safe to assume that between 10% and 20% will go for taxes. Any budgeting that you do ought to take this into account: $600 to $1,200 going to taxes means that the $50 monthly withdrawal check was closer to $40–45.

13   Your Legal Protections

When reaching for a pen to buy shares in a mutual fund, you assume that you are legally protected. Understandably, though, you wonder to what extent. Dim memories and echoes of shenanigans in the stock market will not easily die, nor will that queasy feeling that you are tossing dice with fate. Therefore, it cannot be repeated too often that mutual funds may well be the most carefully regulated part of the entire securities market. I assume that you are like many investors who want a simple, clear, and verifiable explanation of ways in which you are protected, instead of a detailed, historical analysis of government legislation. So I will repeat here, and answer, some of the commonest questions that I have heard prospective fund investors ask.

1. "What about the broker and the dealer? Are they qualified?" Usually, yes. Not just anyone can sell mutual funds. A broker or dealer must earn a license from the National Association of Securities Dealers and his state by passing examinations in the securities investment filed. He must also scrupulously observe Federal and state laws by giving you a prospectus of the fund that he is selling, and the latest quarterly or annual report of the fund in addition to

any approved promotional literature that he wants you to have. In observing the law, he cannot and must not represent the past record of the fund as an indication of its future performance. He cannot guarantee you anything. The Securities and Exchange Commission is watching him, the appropriate state agencies are watching him. So is the National Association of Securities Dealers (which includes most investment banking houses, brokers and dealers in the United States), which has a strict code of ethics for the industry. If he does not follow this code, he can be expelled; so can the firm he represents if it is a party to any misconduct like fraud, deceit or falsehood.

2. "Is it a legal fund?" The Investment Company Act of 1940 requires that a fund register and file with the SEC a comprehensive statement that sets forth the fund's investment policies and purposes, as detailed in Chapter 7. Look at the front page of the prospectus. In prominent capital letters, registration with the SEC is indicated by the statement that the SEC neither approves nor disapproves of the securities or the investment policies of the fund nor does it pass on the adequacy or accuracy of the prospectus. When you see this statement, you know that the fund has been registered. You will also know that the fund has complied with the multiplicity of requirements laid down by the SEC about minimum capitalization ($200,000), organizational structure, clearly defined objectives, and positively stated policies.

When you see a statement on the front page of the prospectus *printed in red,* you will know that the prospectus is a preliminary prospectus (also known as a "red herring"). This prospectus does not constitute an offer of shares in the fund, but merely gives information on the fund. You should carefully compare the preliminary prospectus with the final version to determine whether there have been any alterations, additions, or amendments.

3. "How much am I really being told about the fund?" The law requires that the fund provide you with full, open disclosure of many details of the fund—how it was founded, who will direct it, who will advise it, who will distribute its shares, the professional experience of each member of the board of directors, the amount of the management fee, the number of fund shares held by each member of the board of directors, etc. No broker may sell you shares unless you *first* have a prospectus in your hands. It is your guarantee that the fund, and the broker, are telling you exactly what the fund has told the government. Any deviation from this procedure makes the broker liable to disciplinary action by the National Association of Securities Dealers.

4. "Will the fund use my money in the manner the prospectus describes?" Yes. Once a fund and its policies have been registered with the government, those policies cannot be changed except by approval of you and your fellow shareholders. This is a guarantee that you will get what you pay for; a specific investment policy with specific goals. If you buy into a bond fund of the income variety, the law forbids the management to change it to a performance fund of the "go-go" variety without shareholder consent. If you buy into a diversified common stock growth fund, it cannot be changed by its directors to a preferred stock and bond fund without the consent of a majority of the shareholders.

5. "Will anyone ever get a better deal than I by being able to buy shares cheaper?" The fund is forbidden by law to sell its shares to anyone at a price less than the current net asset value (plus sales charge, if any) as calculated daily. The value of your shares is thus protected against any "undercutting" because of "wholesaling" or other special "deals." Because of the growing number of funds, directors are eager to get their fund's share prices nationally listed in the daily newspapers, thus increasing their

chances of attracting investors. No fund management would prefer the disastrous loss of its potential success and its legal standing if it allowed illegal discounts on purchases. There are legal discounts, however, for quantity purchases and for certain non-profit institutions.

6. "If the government is trying to protect me and other shareholders from another 1929, is there anything else that it says funds cannot do besides lying and making promises?" Yes. The law limits how much a fund can invest in a particular security; for example, if a fund thinks that it has found an unusually promising stock, it might conceivably want to "go for broke" by buying a huge number of shares. The government prohibits the fund's investing more than 5% of its total assets in any individual company's stock. This protects you against any severe loss if that one company were to go bankrupt.

The law also prohibits the fund from holding more than 10% of the securities of any one company, no matter how large. This prevents a fund from controlling a company to the extent that it might actually dictate policy to the managers of that company. What, for example, might happen if a mutual fund owned 51% of the stock of the Standard Oil Company? There are those who argue that a large fund with only 10% of a company's stock may still exercise undue influence on that company to "mend its ways" lest the fund threaten to dump the stock from its portfolio, thereby inducing a drop in the value of that stock. This issue is discussed in Chapter 16.

7. "Does any other group try to protect me as a fund investor?" There is an association of mutual fund management companies, the Investment Company Institute in New York, which tries to enforce an ethical code among its members. It has no legal power, but through its prestige, its knowledge, and its experience, it is very

influential in setting standards of conduct among employees of funds. It publishes a variety of reports, books, and research studies on mutual funds which enhance the reputation of the industry and underscore its continued efforts toward self-improvement. Also, the National Association of Securities Dealers, a non-government body, sets forth strict standards for the conduct of dealers and brokers.

8. "If the fund does not perform well, what can I as a shareholder do?" First, you must recognize that market conditions may be against your fund's performing well. But, if market conditions have been favorable and the fund fares poorly, then a change in the investment advisor may be in order. You and other shareholders approve the contract between the fund and its advisor for a maximum of two years. After that it must be approved each year by a majority of the board of directors, a majority of the independent directors, and by you and your fellow shareholders. The law says that the contract is nontransferable. As a matter of practice, the management companies capitalize the contract. This may seriously dilute the influence of shareholders.

9. "If I receive dividends and capital gains distributions, will the fund explain them?" Each fund must send you an annual financial statement in which it reports net dividends and net realized capital gains. You will want to use this for income tax purposes. The annual (or quarterly) report also lists for you the changes the fund has made in its portfolio holdings: the securities it sold and bought during the year. It may prove revealing to see which issues the fund sold and which it acquired.

10. "Does the government know what the fund does each year or is there only a one-shot registration with the SEC?" Every fund must file each year a *sixty-four* page form that covers every aspect

of its operations—expenses, portfolio turnover rates, salaries, etc. It is extraordinarily detailed. The disclosures required are so complete that the Investment Company Institute describes the operations of funds as taking place "in a goldfish bowl."

11. "May the fund ever refuse to redeem my shares?" The only time a fund may suspend redemption of your shares is when trading on the New York Stock Exchange is restricted or the Exchange is closed, or when the SEC permits suspension or declares an emergency. Some funds reserve the right—if their boards of directors consider it in the best interests of their shareholders and with the present approval of the SEC—to pay the redemption price in whole or in part by a distribution of shares from the portfolio of the fund in lieu of cash. Each investor is properly reminded in the prospectus that the value of the shares on redemption may be more or less than the investor's cost, depending on the net asset value of the fund's shares at the time redemption is requested.

12. "I have never seen this particular fund advertise. Why?" In 1950, the SEC established strict rules about fund advertising and promotional literature. Those rules are enforced by the N.A.S.D., to which funds submit advertising brochures and other sales materials for approval. The SEC regulations on advertising are so severe that they have been called "tombstone" requirements: a fund may only identify itself by name; describe in a sentence or two the investment purpose—growth, income, etc.; the type of fund—common stock, diversified stock, bond, etc.; offer you a prospectus; and give its address. Many funds believe that such an ad, like a tombstone, is dull reading and not worth the cost. They prefer to rely on dealers and brokers to spread the word. The strict SEC requirements grew out of excessive advertising in the 1920's in which the most extravagant, unsubstantiated claims were made to the effect that "your investment is fully protected by reliable securities," or "you

need not worry about the certainty of the profitable future of these companies."

Not only must fund advertisements be limited to a few facts describing the fund; its prospectus and promotional brochures must also categorically state that the fund cannot guarantee any future results based on past results, that the value of the investment may drop as well as rise, and that no figure from the past should be interpreted as any indication of the future.

13. "Am I liable for any taxes owed by the fund?" A mutual fund pays no income taxes provided that it complies with the requirements of the Internal Revenue Service concerning "regulated investment companies." The major requirement is that the fund must distribute to you and the other shareholders at least 90% of its *net* income, in addition to *all* capital gains. In brief, the fund does not make and keep a profit; you, the shareholder, are given the profits and you pay the taxes. The mutual fund acts as a "conduit" through which these monies pass.

14. "How is the sales charge determined?" The maximum sales charge of 9% is fixed by the 1940 Investment Company Act. The charge may range from 0% to 9% and may be variously divided among the custodian bank, the sponsor, the dealer, and the broker. This 9% figure may change, depending on industry decisions and/ or government action.

15. "Are the fund's financial statements verified by the Federal government?" At any time, the SEC may decide to verify the financial report of a fund. If there is any falsification, the fund management company is subject to prosecution just as you are if you falsify your income tax return. Each fund must have its financial statement audited by an independent Certified Public Accountant

before it is filed with the government, and a statement of each such audit must accompany reports submitted.

16. "May the management charge an excessive fee?" The usual management fee is ½ of 1% of the fund's net assets although some are higher. Sometimes a salaried member of the board of directors (the decision-making group) is also a member of the investment advisor company (the advice-giving group) which receives the management fee. The law says that at least 40 percent of the directors of the fund must be independent and completely unaffiliated with the advisor; furthermore, not all directors are salaried. In any case, all salaries and fee figures must be reported to the SEC. They are a matter of public record. In addition, any inquiry that you wish to make about such matters should be directed to the board of directors.

17. "Does the 'top brass' of a fund get special privileges?" The law says that an "insider" cannot buy portfolio securities from the fund or sell securities to the fund. The status and the activities of fund directors and fund advisors is the object of constant scrutiny by government authorities. Another restriction is that one fund cannot buy a substantial block of the shares in another fund.

18. "Would you say that each and every fund is honest?" This is a question about people. The answer is obvious: no Federal or state regulations, no industry-wide self-regulation, and no number of ethical injunctions can ever eliminate *all* abuses. The most important point to ponder is that, functioning within a framework of intricate, widespread legal and moral requirements, no fund can possibly survive for very long if it is dishonest.

19. "I don't understand the role of the custodian bank in the operation of a fund. What is it?" The law prescribes that the securi-

ties and cash owned by a mutual fund must be held by a bank or a member firm of a national securities exchange. Furthermore, any official of the fund having access to the securities and cash must be bonded. The bank, then, is one huge safety deposit box. The bank has nothing to do with management or the supervision of a fund; it is, rather, a custodian or depositary, a safeguard for you against any unauthorized person gaining access either to the cash or the securities of a fund.

20. "Can I trust the accuracy of the data that the broker gives me?" All the statistical details, graphs, charts, and sums must be accurate. Fundamental errors are subject to severe penalties. Though you need not suspect the accuracy of the fund's data, you must be alert to the interpretation of the data and how that data would compare with that of funds with similar investment policies and similar objectives.

The answers to these typical questions ought to reinforce your conclusion that you are legally protected in mutual funds. I can only begin to suggest here the numerous requirements that the government has placed on the funds to safeguard your investment. Furthermore, the vigilance with which the government watches the fund industry, and the diligence with which the industry regulates itself, should allay most of your fears of a recurrence of 1929. Out of the tragedies of that year and the ensuing depression, a new day dawned.

The Turning Point: 1933

The seed of all the protections that you enjoy in mutual funds was planted by the Federal Securities Act of 1933. The mood of Congress and the American people demanded that there be full disclosure of the nature of any security sold in interstate commerce. Then, as now, the government did not approve or disapprove of the security, nor did it forbid the selling of speculative securities. But starting in that year, it did require that an investor be fully informed about what he is buying. Any investment company selling shares to the public was required to give each customer an accurate prospectus and to file it with the SEC. Here, Congress was thinking of new securities, ones that had never been issued before.

The Second Milestone: 1934

The Federal Securities Exchange Act of 1934 went further, reflecting the determination of Congress and the people to strengthen protection for the investor. That act dealt with the buying and the selling of outstanding securities. It was the source of today's stringent regulation of every facet of the stock exchange. Under the law it became a federal crime to defraud or deceive any person purchasing a security, either through the stock exchange, interstate commerce, or the mails.

The Bill of Rights for Mutual Funds: The Investment Company Act of 1940

During the mid-thirties the SEC was stern in its attitude toward the few existing mutual funds; it was deeply concerned over the public's understanding of them. The agency proposed a strict legislative act governing funds and then invited industry spokesmen to Washington. For years there were public hearings, committee reports, special investigations and joint conferences between government representatives and industry leaders. They hammered away at drafting a bill that would satisfy both sides. The Act that emerged had the lukewarm support of the SEC. For all practical purposes it was the fund industry that wrote the Act.

Forty-seven pages long, it attempts to leave nothing to chance, nothing to the imagination, and nothing to the unscrupulous charlatan. Its length defies any attempt to comment extensively on it here but it is easily one of the landmarks in the economic history of the United States.

Current government concern over mutual funds has little to do with illegalities, fraud, deceit, conspiracy—some of the glaring abuses against investors that existed in the past. Rather, present concern about funds has to do with the size of sales commissions, the desirability of front-end load contracts, the management fee, and (most important of all) the impact of mutual funds on the rise and decline of the value of securities in the stock market. These are all pressing questions but none of them smacks of conspiratorial schemes against you. Men of experience and intelligence differ on how these issues ought to be resolved.

14 The Management Fee

Before you make any yearly profit on your mutual fund shareholdings, you will pay usually a ½ of 1% management fee, or 5 cents on each dollar of the net asset value per share. One of the major criticisms of mutual funds is that this management fee is unreasonably high. In its 1966 report, *Public Policy Implications of Investment Company Growth,* the SEC recommended lowering mutual fund management fees, though it set no specific figure. The Commission held that investors in mutual funds have not enjoyed the reduced costs which usually characterize large business enterprises. The Commission felt that if the public is to benefit from the economies that usually accompany size, some outside authority should determine the management fee.

The Commission based its recommendation on a finding that effective competition, which normally restrains prices, does not operate in the area of mutual fund management fees. Funds cannot find reasonably inexpensive investment advice. Furthermore, the buying public neither knows very much about the fees charged to mutual funds nor considers the question of management fees because it is too preoccupied with other concerns as investors. The Commission also concluded that neither the unaffiliated directors of a fund nor the shareholders—through court action—have any significant restraining influence on management fees.

Understandably, the mutual fund industry is bitterly opposed to any interference from some outside authority in setting management fees. A vitally important issue that involves every fund investor, it is bound to erupt this year and next, generating heated debate and possibly Congressional legislation. As an actual or potential investor in mutual funds, you ought to give the question very careful thought.

Key Terms

To thread your way through the issue, study the following terms:

1. *externally managed fund* employs a separate investment advisor;
2. *internally managed fund* is managed by some members of its own board of directors and by some affiliated members of the fund management company;
3. *unaffiliated director* is an independent member of the board of directors of a fund; he has no connection with the investment advisory service and no financial interest in the fund;
4. *noninvestment company client* is any client—other than a fund—that is served by an investment advisor.

The Wharton Report Findings

The Wharton Report examined the management fee rates for externally managed funds, for internally managed funds, and for noninvestment company clients of investment advisors. Of a total of 163 advisors surveyed, at least 54 managed the assets of other clients as well as of mutual funds.

The study found that the management fee rates of externally managed funds were "significantly higher" than those for internally managed funds. It also found that the fees were "very much higher" than those charged to noninvestment company clients with comparable assets. Furthermore, it found that the fee rates for the externally managed funds did not change much regardless of the asset size of the fund.

Cost in relation to fees. The Wharton team asked, "Can the greater amount and the lesser flexibility of the fees charged to externally managed funds be explained by the *services* of the investment advisor or by the *costs* incurred by the investment advisor?" Since services provided to both internally and externally managed funds are similar, the costs were closely examined. It was found that

1. mutual fund assets cost less for investment advisors to manage than the assets of other clients;
2. costs for internally managed funds were "significantly lower" than for externally managed funds;
3. costs of external investment advisor services fell substantially as the size of fund assets increased;
4. the sharpest decrease in cost ratios was experienced by the investment advisors who served only mutual fund clients;
5. the decrease in cost ratio was not as great for the investment advisors who managed both mutual fund and noninvestment company assets.

The critical conclusion from the entire study was this: *the assets of the average noninvestment company client cost more per dollar to manage than do mutual fund assets.* In contrast, the costs of managing mutual funds fall sharply as asset size increases. Therefore, the explanation for the higher and less flexible management fee rates charged to mutual funds must be found elsewhere than in costs incurred or services rendered. In brief, there is a discrepancy between the cost of managing a fund and the fee charged for managing a fund, a discrepancy that may fairly be described as consisting of profit. The critics feel that this profit is too large.

Industry Justification for Its Profit

The commonest response of the mutual fund industry concentrates on whether an individual shareholder could obtain a lower management fee rate in another investment. It argues that a shareholder could not do better elsewhere. But the critic insists that this argument does not meet the central issue squarely, claiming that if a mutual fund is a single account, managed as a single investment, why do its management fees fail to reflect actual cost differences as they do for noninvestment clients?

A second question the critic raises is this: Is the responsibility of a fund director discharged when he has demonstrated that the shareholder, whose interests he represents, has no better option? Presumably, the director of the fund observes that expense ratios decline as assets grow. He knows that there is a scaled rate for noninvestment clients and the rate charged to a mutual fund. Still, he generally concludes that the management fee rate is satisfactory because the mutual fund shareholder could not do better elsewhere.

The Industry View of Management Fee Rates

Most industry spokesmen agree on the proposition that management fees should be "reasonable." As a corollary, many of these men favor a reduction in management fees through some form of sliding scale as fund assets grow. But these same spokesmen are adamant against having management fees controlled, directly or indirectly, by any government agency. They insist that remedies and safeguards to control excessive fees already exist. They offer a variety of arguments, some of which we now examine.

First, there is the nature of the investment advisor's business. The professional management of other people's money, for individual investors or through a mutual fund, is a personal service business. It is competitive, with no monopoly and no limited right of entry. There is full disclosure of all costs at the time of purchase and four times each year. An investor has a wide choice of mutual funds with differing objectives, investment policies, and management fees ranging from ⅛ of 1% to 1%.

Second, there is no need for governmental regulation of management fees. Mutual fund directors are acutely aware of their responsibilities, evidenced by reductions in fees by many large funds. One tabulation in 1968 showed that of those funds whose assets were $100 million or more, the average management fee was 37/100ths of 1%. Many funds charged less.

Third, if shareholders become dissatisfied with what their fund directors are doing, they have recourse to the courts for a decision on whether or not their fund's management fees are excessive. The long period of lawsuits throughout the fund industry's history, the Wharton Report, and the SEC's "Public Policy" Report have made all directors very conscious of their responsibilities and the risks involved if they fail to meet them.

The Industry's Criteria for a Reasonable Management Fee

The major criterion for a reasonable management fee, says the industry, ought to be the record of fund performance: how well the fund has done in accordance with stated objectives and investment policies. If the performance is good, the management contract should be renewed. If performance is lacking, the fund should find a new investment advisor with a good record and submit the choice to fund shareholders for approval. The ability demonstrated in the management of the fund would seem to be the important consideration.

The second criterion for a reasonable management fee ought to be the quality and depth of the management organization as reflected by its ability to continuously provide competent management of your money despite changing times and turnover in personnel.

Some Additional Arguments by Industry

The fund industry rejects as inappropriate the SEC suggestion that mutual fund management fees ought to be compared with the management fees of pension funds. However, the industry does believe that a comparison with bank charges on their common trust funds *is* appropriate. For the management of a $5,000 trust fund, a bank generally charges 5%; for a $10,000 trust fund, the charge is 2½%. Only at $100,000 is the bank's charge comparable to the ⅜ of 1% to ½ of 1% charged as a management fee by most funds.

In addition, the fund industry can point to specific funds that have grown phenomenally while their management fees have undergone noticeable reductions. They are exceptional, but the industry contends that they are evidence that competition *does* work to lower management fees.

Some Critical Rejoinders to the Mutual Fund Industry

First, the critic reminds the industry that the "unaffiliated director" is supposed to be the chief safeguard provided by the Investment Company Act of 1940 against the domination of a mutual fund by investment advisors or managers. An independent director is supposed to protect the shareholder against any tendency of the management toward excessive fees. Section 15(c) states, in part,

"It shall be unlawful for any registered investment company having a board of directors to enter into, renew, or perform any contract or agreement, written or oral . . . unless the terms of such contract or agreement and any renewal thereof have been approved (1) by a majority of the directors who are not parties to such contract or agreement or affiliated persons of any such party . . ."

Who selects the "unaffiliated director"? As one lawyer put it, "The men who need to be watched pick the watchdogs to watch them." True, the unaffiliated director must not own stock in the fund nor may he be an officer or director of the fund's advisor, management company, or underwriter. But the human inclination of directors is to choose "one of ours"—an independent director who is friendly, cooperative, and of the same predisposition as the other directors. This can lead to mischief. One prominent member of a well-known law firm has stated:

"I have had fourteen investment company cases and fourteen sets of depositions and/or cross examinations of the independent directors, and in not one single case did any unaffiliated director ever respond 'Yes' to this type of question: 'When your fund grew from $100 million to $600 million, did you ever give any thought to making a comparison between your half of one percent fees and somebody else's fees?'

" 'No.'

"Did you ever give any thought to an internal management, á la (name of another fund)?

" 'No.'

"Did you ever once suggest that when the fund got to be over a billion dollars—in one or two of the cases I had—perhaps a reduction from one-half percent to seven-sixteenths of one percent, or any other minute fraction?

"Answer: 'No' and I mean the uniform answer.

"The answer is that the realities are, as the SEC's report well recognizes, that you can't count on the unaffiliated director. There's no point in condemning him and using harsh epithets. The fact is that in real life the unaffiliated director never has initiated a movement for a reduction of fees.

"I don't want to overstate the argument. There have been times when fees have been reduced, but that's in spite of the unaffiliated directors. That's when, because of conditions, perhaps, of competition, or what have you, the management—the advisor—has determined that it would be good business to reduce the fee. That's not happened very often, but it has sporadically."

Second, critics of fund management fees insist that performance should be taken into account in determining the fee. A few funds use some related performance standard (like the Dow Jones Average) but the vast majority do not. The Wharton Report studied fee rates over a number of years and found no correlation whatsoever between rates and performance. The critic asks, "Why shouldn't funds use some performance-related standards for establishing fees?" After all, he says, an investor in a fund has a performance objective, taking a smaller risk in a balanced fund or a greater risk in a go-go fund. Why shouldn't the management fee hinge on the extent to which that performance is realized? The critic maintains that it is sound economics. Besides, rarely, if ever, have independent directors decided that the management had done such a poor job that it ought to be "fired" and a new management hired. This is very unfair to shareholders, the critic believes.

In this connection, the same lawyer quoted above has also said:

". . . the investment company fellows have for the first time introduced this brand new concept of giving management a percentage of brick and masonry, that is, of all assets, without regard to whether they are making productive use of them. This is a brand new conception: if you are big enough, your reward goes to you merely because of your size, even though your investor may be suffering great losses, or not making profits, and I think conceptually, philosophically, that's a completely wrong approach."

Third, the critic asserts that as things stand now, when individual shareholders have claimed the existence of an excessive management fee in a fund and have taken the matter to court, the action has generally been nonsuited or dismissed by the judge. Even though the court may have felt that the fees were excessive, it has also felt bound to follow the *presumed will* of a majority of the shareholders who ratified the fee, a meaningless ratification because shareholders rarely read carefully what they vote on. The critic agrees with the SEC recommendation that the court should *not* be bound by shareholders' stated approval of the management fee in question if the court finds that such fees are excessive.

The standards for "excessive" fees or "unreasonable" fees which a court of equity would use would have to be worked out, presumably with the help of the SEC. While not an easy problem, continues the critic, it is no more difficult than the present helplessness of shareholders who have no significant voice in determining the management fee or in getting rid of a poorly performing management.

Finally, the critic says that there are serious conflicts of interest in mutual fund management structure. The first, already mentioned, is between the unaffiliated director's representing the shareholders on the fund's board of directors and his loyalty to those affiliated members of the board who appointed him. The second is between the investment advisor's being a fiduciary to the stockholders of the fund and at the same time serving its own self-interest by getting the highest fee possible from the board of directors. Third, when it turns out that some of the affiliated directors are the same as some of the investment advisors, the conflicts between self-interest and fiduciary responsibility are really strained.

Industry Fears

Industry is less worried about the criticisms explained above than by what they might lead to. If the independent directors of a fund are not in the best position to decide on reasonable management fees, who is? Any other alternative smacks of rate regulation by government and, to this, industry is strongly opposed. It believes that the independent directors are the best judges of a reasonable fee, based on their expectations from the investment advisor and on his performance.

Many fund managers are leery of necessarily tying the management fee to fund performance because it may encourage excessive speculation. Good judgment and intelligent caution in portfolio changes might give way to a "race" for performance which is not in the best interest of the shareholders. If shareholders want a speculative fund, that's one thing, but the great majority of funds are not go-go, and they boast that their sound record is based on prudent investing. Tying management fee to performance would be a dangerous precedent.

Another danger in deciding to penalize or to change management because of "poor" performance lies in the realities of any growing business: there is often a long period of time when there are difficulties in getting a fund started and in making money as the fund grows. Until volume is significantly achieved, poor management performance cannot be assumed. It may take years before excellent management is able to make money. One fund was started in 1929. By 1940 it had grown to $5 million but it had made no money. By 1945 it had grown to $15 million but it still had not made any money. Not until the late 1940's, achieving real volume, did the management's efforts become profitable. A good manager does not necessarily always make a profit.

Fund men fear, also, that the SEC may be seeking rate regulation by the threat of litigation. What does court action really mean? It means the by-passing of the actions of unaffiliated directors who approved a contract that they considered reasonable. The court would use its own judgment about the equity of a contract approved by presumably disinterested directors. In other words, the court or the SEC may try to exercise a function which is usually carried out by the directors of corporations.

As for the "conflict of interest" inherent in fund structure, the industry flatly asserts empirical evidence to the contrary. If there are unaffiliated directors who don't represent the shareholders' interests and who do not exercise independent judgment, they are in a minority. Furthermore, if and when a director is simultaneously a member of the investment advisor, the government's watchdogs and industry's self-policing militate against any irregularities being perpetrated on shareholders.

As a present or potential shareholder, keep well informed and give continued, serious thought to the power of the unaffiliated director, the fiduciary responsibility of directors and investment advisors; the desirability of internalizing management; government rate regulation; and problems emerging from the relationships among affiliated directors, investment advisors, and unaffiliated directors.

It is vitally important that you avoid sweeping generalizations regarding "fund managers" (or directors) when and if alleged abuses are discovered in any particular fund. You owe it to yourself to remain as well informed as you can about the management of your fund (or funds), always remembering the efforts of the fund industry to regulate itself. You should develop a philosophy of what is a "reasonable management fee" and do whatever you can to implement that philosophy as a mutual fund shareholder.

15   Selecting Your Funds

If you want to be a contented mutual fund investor, you must first decide whether you are interested primarily in *growth* of your investment ("capital appreciation"), *income* from your investment ("dividend yield and capital gains"), or *stability* of your investment ("capital preservation"), or some combination of these three objectives weighted according to your preference. Only after you make this basic decision are you ready to select the mutual fund(s) best for you. Great dissatisfaction and disillusionment may await you if you are a conservative investor who picks an aggressively managed, common stock growth fund that declines as sharply as it rises, or if you are an aggressive investor who picks a very conservative balanced fund that never gives you any "action."

The General Types of Funds

Funds range from the most conservative to the most speculative. The most conservative seek higher dividends while minimizing appreciation and risk. Others emphasize growth, with increased risk. Among existing funds there is a large range of many combinations and emphases, the distinctions sometimes being very subtle. There are major categories within which the above three basic investment objectives are sought. These major types include the following:

1. *Bond and Preferred Stock Funds.* These funds aim for stability and predictable, fixed amount of dividend income. Variations in this category depend on the relative emphasis on income or stability. They are one of the most popular types of funds among people desiring an income.

2. *Balanced Funds.* These funds invest in bonds, preferred stocks, and common stocks. It is a normal practice for fund managers, in market declines, to sell their common stock holdings and increase their bond and preferred stock holdings. They adopt an opposite course when the market rises. Varying the ratio of commons to preferreds and bonds is one way to achieve investment objectives of a fund.

3. *Common Stock Funds.* The most numerous of all funds, these invest almost entirely in common stocks, sacrificing the stability of preferred stocks and bonds in return for growth possibilities and capital gains. When the market rises, they tend to fare well, and vice versa. There are many different combinations within common stock funds. Some seek special situations, or new industries, or solid, well-established companies. A careful reading of a fund's prospectus will help you pin down more precisely how the fund may be conveniently classified in terms of its aims and portfolio policies.

Specific Categories of Funds

Exact categorization of funds is impossible. Classifications are necessarily arbitrary and cannot be interpreted as meaning that all funds under the same heading have identical purposes or policies. However, in broad objectives, policies, and types, funds may be conveniently grouped. Examining the ways in which funds are grouped by various publications, you will discover many similarities. The groupings suggested by *FundScope* will be as helpful and accurate as any that you will find. *Forbes* magazine, Wiesenberger's *Investment Companies,* and Johnson Company's *Investment Company Charts* are useful, too. Remember that the most complete explanation of a fund's policies and objectives is found in the fund's prospectus (see Chapter 7).

I. GROWTH FUNDS

These funds try to achieve maximum capital appreciation over the long-term. These are almost always heavily invested (up to as high as 95%) in promising common stocks. There are four major kinds of growth funds.

1. *Diversified Common Stocks* (dcs) These funds invest in promising common stocks. Their reputation, record, and probable future performance make them attractive if your investment objective is growth of capital.

2. *Semi-Diversified* (sd) These are often called "performance" or "go-go" funds. They are probably the fastest-growing funds, seeking the stocks of little-known but promising companies. They also try to uncover companies on the recovery route or companies in "special situations." The managers of these funds may use a wide variety of speculative investment methods and seek frequent portfolio turnover. This type of fund is for the aggressive investor, able to assume greater than average risks and willing to accept sharp declines.

3. *Specialized Funds* (spl) These funds invest primarily in one industry or one area, like utilities, nuclear energy, electronics, or oceanography.

4. *Specialized Insurance Funds* (ins) These funds invest in the stocks of various kinds of insurance companies (such as life, accident and health, fire and casualty) as well as in companies whose principal business is owning and managing insurance companies. The growth potential of insurance company stocks is great as is evidenced by the recent "come-back" in the market.

II. Canadian and/or International Securities

The portfolios of these funds are heavily invested in foreign securities. The primary purpose is growth (capital appreciation).

III. Growth, with Income

These funds are for the investor who wants growth of his investment but not at the sacrifice of income. He would probably want to take his dividends in cash and have the capital gains distributions reinvested in additional shares. There are two major types of these funds.

1. *Diversified Common Stocks* (dcs) The diversification in the portfolio will be primarily in common stocks through most market periods.

2. *Flexibly Diversified* (fd) Management may change the common stock diversification in this fund more readily to other types of investments such as bonds or preferred stocks to lessen risks in uncertain market periods.

IV. Income and Growth

These funds try to achieve income and growth about equally. As explained in III above, there are two major types, (dcs) and (fd).

V. Growth, Income, and Stability

These are the "balanced funds" that seek investment goals in some combination:

1. *Growth-Income, Stability* (G-I-S) This type fund seeks growth of principal and growth of income over the years (at the beginning both growth and income may be low) through investing in promising companies with strong growth potential. At the same time, the fund will seek as much stability as possible.

2. *Income-Growth, Stability* (I-G-S) This type fund seeks income growth, and growth of capital (at the beginning, both income and growth may be low) while maintaining as much stability as possible. The investments will be in well-established and promising companies.

3. *Stability-Income, Growth* (S-I-G) This type fund seeks stability of an investment while achieving regularity of dividend income. Hopefully, growth of capital may occur but it is not one of the primary objectives.

VI. Income Funds, Flexibly Diversified (fd)

These funds seek income, primarily, but at some risk to the investment. They diversify their portfolios among investments that promise the best dividend income, particularly preferred stocks, "blue chips," or common stocks which are less speculative.

VII. Bond and Preferred Stock Funds

As their name implies, these funds are probably the least aggressive.

1. *Stability-Income* (S-I) These funds seek preservation of capital and stability of income.

2. *Income-Stability* (I-S) These funds seek income while trying to maximize stability.

3. *Income* (I) These funds aim at income primarily, at some risk to the stability of the investment.

Select the Type of Fund That Meets Your Needs

Carefully look over the seven major types of funds. Which one comes closest to your purposes? And how do you want the fund to pursue its goal—aggressively or conservatively? It may be that you can afford to invest in a "package" of funds in which case you can select two or three types that provide investment balance. Otherwise, zero in on the one type that best meets your goals, and diversify within that type.

Use More Than a Single Criterion in Choosing a Fund

If you select a fund entirely on the basis of its performance results, you may be making a serious mistake. In conjunction with performance, you must consider the fund's investment objective, policy, type, and record. If a fund states that its primary objective is stability, then its relative performance should be judged by how little it loses in declining markets and not by how much it gains in rising markets. Also, remember that a relatively stable asset value denies you the opportunity to make purchases of shares at a "bargain" (when the market is down), and consequently your "dollar-cost average" will be higher. With over 300 funds now available, and many more on the way, making choices would seem to be an insurmountable task. This is not true. Once you have decided on your objective, you may then consider the fund that falls into that category.

Investigate Specific Fund Ratings and Performances

If you wish to proceed on your own, go to a public library and find fund ratings and rankings in *Forbes'* annual August issue or *FundScope's* annual April issue. You may also wish to consult Johnson's annual *Investment Company Charts* or Wiesenberger's *Investment Companies.*

If you wish to proceed with a broker, locate one through your accountant, a family friend, or the Yellow Pages. Tell him the type fund that you want and express your interest in rankings and ratings. Ask for prospectuses, shareholder reports, and other pertinent literature. Don't let yourself be intimidated by hard-sell. Many brokers will avoid that. After all, your satisfaction means money in their pockets through your initial investment and through your subsequent purchases. Most brokers sell many different funds; some brokers deal exclusively in one fund; some funds have their own "captive" sales organizations. Be constantly aware of the relationship between the broker and the fund that he is recommending so that you can assess intelligently the breadth of his objectivity and the quality of his analysis.

Use Basic Market Periods When You Study a Fund's History

If you are interested primarily in growth and capital appreciation in your investment, study the fund's record in rising market years 1961, 1963, 1964, 1965, 1967, and 1968. If you are interested primarily in relative price-stability (capital preservation), study the fund's record in the severely declining market years 1962 and 1966. If you want a combination of growth-income-stability, examine a fund's record in *both* rising and declining years; study also the fund's current yield and then check the fund's 1, 5, and 10-year dividend record. Remember, the newer the fund, the less his-

torical data will be available, so it is doubly important to secure as much information, opinion, and comparative data as you can.

When you study fund performance, be sure to use prospectuses if you can (see Part III, Chapter 7).

Study Fund Operating Expenses

Late in 1968 the editor of *FundScope,* Allan Silver, pointed out that there is little mention of operating expenses "from the investor's point of view" among magazines and books on mutual funds. Moreover, publications that do mention the subject usually give operating expenses *as a percent of each fund's total assets* rather than *as a percent of a fund's investment income* which should interest you more. Lamenting the lack of meaningful analysis and statistics on operating costs of mutual funds, *FundScope* devoted its November, 1968, issue to factual tabulations of the operating costs of 238 mutual funds.

Operating expenses for a fund include the following: fees for the management company, custodian, registrar, stock transfer, dividend disbursement, directors, attorneys' and accountants' reports and notices to shareholders; and miscellaneous operating costs. *FundScope* tabulated the relationship between these expenses and the asset size of each fund and the operating expenses and income of each fund. It tabulated fund expenses as % ratios of assets and as % ratios of income. Its two major statistical findings were as follows:

1. The median operating expense in terms of % *of net assets* was 0.68% ($6.80 per year per thousand dollars of your investment). The range was wide, from the fund having the lowest expense ratio of 0.17% ($1.70 per year per thousand dollars) to the fund with the highest expense ratio of 7.16% ($71.60 per year per thousand dollars).

2. The median operating expense in terms of *percentage of net*

income was 24.8% ($248 per thousand dollars of your investment). Again, there was a wide variation, from the fund with the lowest expense of 5.4% ($54 per thousand dollars of your investment) to the fund with the highest expense of 658.4% ($6,584 per thousand dollars of your investment).*

Generalizations about Operating Expenses

With a wealth of data among many different sizes and types of funds, *FundScope* came to the following conclusions which may help to guide you in selecting funds.

a. *Relationship between fund size and operating expenses.* There is a definite relationship between the size of a fund and its expenses, with size favoring a *low* expense ratio. Large size, however, is *not,* by itself, an indication of low expense ratios. Also, a fund's investment objective may determine its expense ratio. There is a tendency for a high expense ratio to be matched by relatively small size, though a number of large funds have a low expense-asset ratio.

b. *Relationship between fund expenses and net income.* Of those funds with the lowest expense-income ratio, most are *income* funds. Since growth funds do not aim primarily at income dividends, they will generally have higher expense-income ratios, but *that is to be expected!* Also, those funds with low expense ratios have generally above-average records for capital appreciation, income or stability. However, a high-expense-income ratio is no bar to above-average capital appreciation results.

It would seem clear, then, that if you are seeking capital appreciation, a fund's expense ratio is relatively unimportant and incidental; also, a top fund for income sometimes has a low expense ratio. If you are concerned primarily with current income, give priority to a fund whose expense income ratio is low.

* *FundScope,* November, 1968, p. 37.

Making the Decision

Like thousands, you come to the moment of decision: though you are satisfied that most mutual funds are not overly speculative and are basically long-term investments, your doubt may remain and the question persists: "Shall I invest in mutual funds?" This question may express your natural fear. Although your fear may not be justified, it is very real and ought to be faced. Discussing funds with a large number of investors makes it possible to understand many of their fears. Are the following some that you feel?

1. "What happens if there is a stock market crash, like 1929?" There are two fears here, really. The first is the fear of a crash. Many seasoned financial advisors agree that 35 years of governmental regulation and self-regulation by funds make a "crash" highly unlikely. In terms of our commitments to ourselves and the world, it would be unthinkable. Such an event would not be a Wall Street crash, but a world catastrophe.

The second fear is the loss of your money in the event of a market decline. You might recall the record of mutual funds in the depression thirties as reported by Furst & Sherman in their *Business Decisions That Changed Our Lives:* no mutual fund went into bankruptcy (though there were not many in existence). Because of the diversification of investments in the portfolio of a mutual fund, the chances of bankruptcy are reduced. However, an investment is a risk. A mutual fund is no exception. You *must* face this fact.

There has never been a "run on the market" by the mutual fund shareholder because he seems to hold his securities for investment even during depression periods, using other funds for emergencies. With the growth of very large funds, there is no assurance how fund investors would behave over a period of protracted unemployment and depression.

2. "What if I want to get my money back quickly?" In the first place, you ought *never* to invest in mutual funds unless you have adequately protected yourself with the right kind of life insurance, sufficient cash for all immediate obligations, and a cash reserve for emergencies. In the second place, once you invest in a fund, you may rest assured that the law requires the fund to redeem your shares within 7 days of your written request. Because of delays in the U.S. Postal System, this is becoming more difficult, so don't panic if it takes 10 or 12 days. The redemption privilege is spelled out in detail in the prospectus of each fund.

3. "Are other people really investing? I still feel like a loner." According to the Investment Company Institute, the number of all mutual fund shareholder accounts had risen from 4,879,000 in December, 1960, to 7,904,132 in December, 1967, a gain of 61%. During the same period, the number of mutual fund withdrawal accounts had grown by 725%. These investors received checks totaling an estimated average of $52 million each month during 1967. The withdrawal plans exceeded $4 billion in value, more than 11 times their estimated value of $336 million in 1960. No, you are not a "loner."

4. "I don't like being in a large organization because I'm afraid that I won't know what's going on." If you are in a fund that employs its own dealer organization, the man who sold you your initial investment may call on you periodically (or you can summon him) to review the status of your investment and perhaps make recommendations about modifying it. If you buy through a broker, he will be happy to review the fund's status with you at any time. Furthermore, most funds will send you quarterly and annual reports detailing gains or losses in net asset value per share, dividend declarations, capital gains distributions, and changes in the fund's

portfolio. In these reports the fund's manager usually has some pertinent comments to make about the fund.

The fact is that mutual fund results are an open book in contrast with the completely unknown results achieved by individual investors in the stock market or the results achieved by bank trust departments. No brokerage firms, stock market advisory services, banks or investment counselors ever reveal the actual results achieved by individual investor clients. In contrast, the achievement of mutual fund management is a matter of public record through daily newspaper quotations, fund prospectuses, fund reports, and the publications which rate or rank the funds.

5. "I don't like a broker giving me a hard sell. I'm embarrassed and resentful when he does." If you get into a no-load fund, you won't be dealing with a broker. You will make your own decisions. If you buy through a broker, remember that he wants to earn his commission. Don't hesitate to raise any question and don't rush into signing anything or even consider doing so without asking for all pertinent data and studying it. Be sure to consider the effect of the sales charge on a fund's past performance as well as on the size of your initial investment. It is a violation of SEC regulations for any broker to use as sale literature any investment table or data that ignores sales charges. The broker is also forbidden to represent to you the past performance of a fund as predictive of future performance. The National Association of Securities Dealers enforces these and other SEC regulations among its members.

6. "What happens if I die? Does the fund keep my money?" When a married couple invest in a mutual fund, they may indicate "Joint Tenants With Right of Survivorship" as the way they want their stock certificates filled out. In case of death, ownership goes to the survivor. If there was originally only one owner, his shares

go to the trust beneficiary if he was foresighted enough to set up an "inter-vivos" trust agreement, otherwise it goes into his estate (see Chapter 12). In no case does the money invested ever belong to the fund unless the investor so bequeaths it in his will!

7. "I cannot get rid of the uneasy feeling that mutual funds are speculative, so my money isn't really safe." It is good that you have this feeling. It makes for intelligent caution. Mutual funds do not have the "safety" of a government bond, a savings bank, or a savings and loan association. The impression that a mutual fund is "safe" is unfortunately often created by your friends, acquaintances, or a broker who may pressure you. Don't be easily swayed. Don't invest emergency savings in funds. You must recognize that a mutual fund is basically an investment in the ownership of American business.

8. "I'm not sure that it's moral to invest in mutual funds." Our culture accepts business investment as moral *if* the business is conducted ethically, *if* it operates legally, *if* it contributes to human well-being, *if* the workers share reasonably in the wealth that they produce and *if* management and labor work constructively toward producing goods and services for the general welfare. The economic history of the United States is the story of continuing effort, through education and legislation, to achieve ever-higher standards of business morality.

You can demonstrate that our economic system operates in a superior way to another, given certain criteria. If you reject the operational superiority of capitalism, you simply should not invest any money in a profit-making enterprise. Furthermore, if you do not favor capitalism in a modified form like ours, you should also question many of its other benefits—the comparatively higher standard of living, mass production at low costs, and the advances in medicine, science, education, and technology brought about through research by business and by higher education. Many universities, institutes, and social service organizations depend on American business for financial support. Their endowments and assured income are produced by investments.

16 Toward the Future

We come now to what is easily the biggest single question about mutual funds. It is far more important than load charges, management fees, front-end loads or reciprocal business. The SEC, Congress and the fund industry itself must eventually determine whether the impact of mutual funds upon the stock market is, on balance, beneficial or detrimental to that market. Put another way, "Are mutual funds a blessing or a threat to stock market stability?"

The Steady Increase in Portfolio Turnover Rates

The growing portfolio turnover rates of mutual funds have been severely criticized. In the 1940's and the 1950's large institutions (mutual funds, pension funds, insurance companies, bank trusts, colleges, etc.) did not turn over their portfolios very often. In those days the emphasis was on "buying and holding." As long-term investors, these institutions were considered at that time to be primary factors in market stabilization. The rise and fall of stock prices were caused largely by the many transactions of individual investors or small investor groups.

However, during the past few years these same institutions have been buying and selling more frequently, largely because they are under pressure to make more profits. In 1960, according to the SEC, mutual funds, pension trusts, and insurance companies with combined stockholdings of $44 billion had an average annual portfolio turnover of 9%. By early 1967 the holdings of these institutions had doubled while the portfolio turnover rate had risen to 16%. The stockholdings of these institutions approached $100 billion in 1968, and they were trading approximately 20% of their portfolios. By way of contrast, the average mutual fund portfolio rate of turnover was about 15% in 1962 but had climbed to nearly 32% in 1966. The 1968 average was estimated at roughly 40%, although some funds had a much higher rate of turnover.

The Emphasis on Capital Gains

These increases in the rate of portfolio turnover reflect the increasing emphasis placed on capital gains by all institutional investors. It is perhaps more pronounced among the mutual funds because of their "fishbowl" existence and shareholders' demands for greater returns on their investments. During the 1950's mutual funds distributed about $300 million per year in capital gains to their shareholders. By 1962 that figure had risen to about $500 million and in 1966 it exceeded $1.3 billion. This represents an increase of roughly $1 billion in annual capital gains distributions in about fifteen years! Although specific figures are not available at this writing for the year 1968, it is anticipated that they exceed $1.5 billion.

In the rush to please their shareholders, fund managers increasingly seek those stocks which their analysts expect will rise in price within the near future. They hold such stocks for short-term capital gains, sell them, and begin the cycle anew. Of course, they must pay taxes on such transactions at the short-term capital gains rate. Other fund managers tend to "get on the bandwagon" because they, too, want a "piece of the action" to improve performance results of their funds. When the fund managers, individually and without group consultation, determine that a stock is "fully priced," they begin selling.

When Is a Stock "Fully Priced?"

It is exceptionally difficult for an individual investor to determine when a stock will become "fully priced," meaning when it has reached its highest price level, because fund buying can raise the price of a stock artificially high. When a stock is traded solely on the basis of expectation of future profits, a selling trend can make its price drop quickly. The state of our economy is not so much a determining factor, nor is the condition of the particular corporation whose stock is being traded. It is more the *expectation* of realizing capital gains that motivates some fund managers in many of their investment decisions. Because many fund managers are rewarded partly on their ability to make more money for their shareholders, the desire for performance is somewhat more than academic!

Let us study a brief example of the effect this can have. In a recent two-year period the price of Ford Motor Company stock dropped from $54.38 to $38.50, while that of Northwest Airlines rose from $31.75 to $119.00. What had happened? At the beginning of the period Ford was the sixth largest stockholding of mutual funds while Northwest Airlines ranked forty-ninth. At the end of the 2-year period, Ford was the forty-second largest shareholding of mutual funds, while Northwest Airlines had moved up to fifth! This was essentially a reversal of their respective positions, and was reflected in the market price of their stock.

Fund Monopolization of a Company's Stock

Another pressing problem is this: some mutual funds are so large that one fund manager's decision to trade a particular issue can make a great deal of difference in the availability of that issue. Although the law limits one fund to no more than 10% of a company's stock, a *group* of affiliated funds (all under the same management) could own among them a majority of outstanding shares of an individual issue. By buying large quantities of a particular stock at one time, the management company can save on brokerage fees and can usually negotiate a lower total price. As a result, some groups of funds now own from 10% to 25% of the outstanding shares of an individual company.

The combined ownership of the stock in one company by *all* mutual funds taken together could constitute a majority of the total stock outstanding in that company. This can dwarf the volume of daily trading in that issue. Indeed, mutual funds together may own more stock in a company than would normally be traded on the exchanges in a year's time. This is obviously a very powerful position for the mutual funds to maintain, and it speaks well for the fund management companies that there has been no widescale abuse of this power.

Fund Control of the Management of Companies

Another urgent problem is the possible exercise of control over the management of companies in which the funds invest. Let's say, for example, that Fund XYZ holds 500,000 shares (10%) of Corporation J, which has 5,000,000 shares outstanding. Should the mutual fund management attempt to influence the management policies and decisions of Corporation J? And if so, to what extent? Should the fund exercise voting rights for the fund shareholders, when those shareholders may not be aware of the issues involved? Some would say, "Absolutely not!" But suppose the fund management considers it in the best interests of the fund's shareholders to vote in a particular way? Aren't they then exercising to the best of their ability the fiduciary responsibilities which are theirs? Put another way: "To what extent may, or should, fund management go to protect the interests of their shareholders?" The issues and implications of this problem are explored provocatively in an excellent article by Arthur M. Louis, entitled "The Mutual Funds Have the Votes" (*Fortune,* May, 1967).

The current trend toward domination of the stock market by institutional investors (including funds) will likely continue, especially in view of the new funds which are now becoming established. There are a relatively small number of common stocks listed primarily on the New York Stock Exchange; by 1966, the institutional investors held over 20% of these stocks. By 1968, they held almost 25%. In 1966, institutions were doing about 35% of the trading, which had increased to nearly 40% by 1968. This is the handwriting on the wall for the individual investor. Going it alone, he is going to have greater competition from the professional money managers in the future. Whether the individual investor can survive in the stock market during the years ahead remains to be seen. His chances, however, are getting slimmer every day.

The Influx of New Personnel

Another urgent problem in the future of mutual funds is the avalanche of new sales personnel into the field. Because of the tremendous interest shown by life insurance companies, there will be vast hordes of newly licensed brokers in the very near future. The insurance companies have a ready-made sales force and will be using it effectively in marketing the shares of mutual funds. This concept is valid and will undoubtedly increase the number of fund shareholders far beyond what we now know. However, it must also be emphasized that passing the examination of the National Association of Security Dealers does not by itself qualify anyone to effectively analyze the innumerable alternatives available in mutual fund investing. The process of selection will be doubly important to you in the future, both in finding a responsible broker and in selecting the appropriate fund(s).

Concerning the selection of funds, there is likely to be more than twice the present number within the next five years! There will be mutual funds that may invest exclusively in companies involved with technical processes and techniques which are not even imaginable today. Technological advances will make your opportunities all the greater and unless you carefully watch what you are doing, a great deal riskier as well. In addition to those funds being organized by life insurance companies, there will probably be funds sponsored by savings and loan associations, banks, credit unions, trade unions, fraternal organizations, etc. As one comedian put it, "Everybody wants to get into the act!" The way it looks, everyone probably will.

SOURCES OF INFORMATION ON MUTUAL FUNDS

MAGAZINES

1. *California Financial Journal,* 2220 South Hill Street, Los Angeles, California 90007. A weekly, the leading financial journal for the west coast, and the official publication for the California Society of Registered Representatives.
2. *Forbes,* 60 5th Avenue, New York, New York 10011. A semi-monthly with a regular column, "The Funds." Rates the stability performance of funds in its annual August issue.
3. *Fortune,* 540 North Michigan Avenue, Chicago, Illinois 60611. Monthly with a regular column entitled "Personal Investing" that sometimes features mutual fund subjects.
4. *FundScope,* 1800 Avenue of the Stars, Century City, Los Angeles, California 90067. Performance comparisons each month and annually. An excellent source of data, rankings, and ratings of mutual funds, particularly the annual April issue. Helpful articles on many aspects of investment techniques. Reprints of back issues available.
5. *Investment Dealers' Digest,* 150 Broadway, New York, New York 10038. Fortnightly contains news and information on mutual funds, with an annual mutual fund directory in September.
6. *Investment Sales Monthly,* Box 1897, Coral Gables, Florida 33134. A magazine on investments that is used by many registered representatives and brokers, with much material on mutual funds.
7. *Trusts & Estates,* 132 West 31st Street, New York, New York

10001. A monthly containing "Index of Mutual Funds" and other articles about mutual funds.

NEWSLETTERS AND NEWSPAPERS

1. *Aggressive Growth Fund Reports,* Charles H. Thomas, Inc., P.O. Box 667, Los Altos, California 94022. A monthly, with detailed, statistical ratings of performance or "go-go" funds: current news and views, interim progress reports, ratings, analyses, tables and charts, and other basic information.
2. *Barron's,* 200 Burnett Road, Chicopee, Massachusetts 01020. Weekly developments in finance, industry, securities markets, politics, and world events with a view toward helping an investor make decisions.
3. *California Business,* 1060 Crenshaw Boulevard, Los Angeles, California 90019. A weekly newspaper dealing exclusively with business and financial news in the west.
4. *Growth Fund Guide,* P.O. Box 2109, Long Beach, California 90801. A monthly guide to "dynamic growth funds," provides data, charts, statistics and performance analyses of funds of the "go-go" variety.
5. *Mutual Affairs,* newsletter published by Arthur Wiesenberger Services Division of Nuveen Corporation, 61 Broadway, New York, New York 10006. A monthly, relating to the broad spectrum of the investment company field and its various components.
6. *Mutual Fund Buyer's Guide,* Point Lookout, New York 11569. Gives computerized monthly "performance listings" which rank funds. Primarily a guide for selecting performance funds offering capital growth potential.
7. *Mutual Fund Reporter,* c/o Investors Research, P.O. Box 8415, Station F, Atlanta, Georgia 30306. A monthly newsletter devoted exclusively to studies and analyses of developments and performance among mutual funds.
8. *The New York Times,* 229 West 43rd Street, New York, New York 10036. Daily and Sunday regularly carries detailed news stories and articles on developments in the mutual fund industry. Excellent coverage of the impact of mutual funds on the stock market, of Congressional concerns and studies of mutual funds, of SEC activities relating to mutual funds and helpful stories on the workings of funds.
9. *Performance Guide Publications,* P.O. Box 2604, Palos Verdes Peninsula, California 90274. A weekly newsletter which reports and analyzes the performance data of growth funds.

10. *The Wall Street Journal,* 30 Broad Street, New York, New York 10004. One of the most widely respected financial dailies in the United States. A source of stock market data, stories of economic trends and developments, helpful analyses of the country's financial affairs and frequent news stories and articles on mutual funds.

11. *United Business Service Report,* 210 Newbury Street, Boston, Massachusetts 02116. Concise weekly forecasts of stock market trends based on opinions of financial and economic observers with occasional reports and recommendations on mutual funds.

SPECIAL AND STANDARD REFERENCE WORKS

1. *Forbes,* annual August issue. 540 North Michigan Avenue, Chicago, Illinois 60611. Ranks and rates the stability performance of mutual funds. (See Chapter 5.)

2. *FundScope,* annual April issue. 1800 Avenue of the Stars, Century City, Los Angeles, California 90067. Rankings and ratings of mutual funds and much statistical data on individual funds. (See Chapter 5.)

3. *Investment Companies,* annual publication of Arthur Wiesenberger Services Division of Nuveen Corporation, 61 Broadway, New York, New York 10006. Reports on mutual fund management results in a variety of categories. (See Chapter 5.)

4. *Investment Company Charts,* annual publication by Hugh A. Johnson & Company, Rand Building, Buffalo 3, New York. Contains 10-year performance records of most mutual funds and much data for performance comparisons. One of the most widely used reference works in the industry.

5. *Mutual Funds,* annual statistical summary of mutual fund data by the Investment Company Institute, 61 Broadway, New York, New York 10006.

6. *Mutual Fund Directory,* published semiannually by *Investment Dealers' Digest,* 150 Broadway, New York, New York 10038. Factual information on all open-end funds in the United States and Canada.

SPECIAL PUBLISHERS

1. American Institute for Economic Research, Great Barrington, Massachusetts 01230. Publishes books on investments and insurance.

2. Arthur Wiesenberger Services Division of Nuveen Corporation, 61 Broadway, New York, New York 10006. Publishes many

financial books and advisory services. Free catalogue on request.

3. Capital Planning Corporation, 337 West Lockwood Avenue, St. Louis, Missouri 63119. Publishes books on mutual funds and life insurance. President Robert E. Kahroff is available for speaking engagements.

4. Institute for Business Planning, Inc., 2 West 13th Street, New York, New York 10011. Publishes financial advisory books.

5. Insurance Planning Corporation, 2934 Fulton Avenue, Sacramento, California 95821. Publishes books on mutual funds and life insurance.

6. Investment Company Institute, 61 Broadway, New York, New York 10006. Publishes many books, pamphlets, and statistical reports on mutual funds. Write for free catalogue.

BOOKS AND SPECIAL STUDIES ON MUTUAL FUNDS

1. *A Comprehensive Study—The Mutual Fund Shareholder.* New York: Investment Company Institute, revised annually.
2. *A Study of Mutual Funds,* prepared for the Securities and Exchange Commission by the Wharton School of Finance and Commerce, the University of Pennsylvania, Report of the Committee on Interstate and Foreign Commerce, U.S. House of Representatives. House Report Number 2274, 87th Congress, 2nd Session, 1962.
3. Barnes, Leo. *Your Buying Guide to Mutual Funds and Investment Companies.* Larchmont, New York: American Research Council, 1960.
4. Baum, Daniel J., and Stiles, Ned B. *The Silent Partners: Institution Investors and Corporate Control.* Syracuse, New York: Syracuse University Press, 1965.
5. Bullock, Hugh. *The Story of Investment Companies.* New York: Columbia University Press, 1960.
6. *Conference On Mutual Funds.* University of Pennsylvania Law School. Philadelphia: University of Pennsylvania Law Review, Vol. 115, No. 5, March, 1967.
7. Doane, C. Russell. *Investment Trusts and Funds From the Investor's Point of View.* Great Barrington, Massachusetts: American Institute for Economic Research, 1966.
8. Dunton, Loren. *How to Sell More Mutual Funds, Especially to*

Women. New York: Echo House, 1967 (subsidiary of Investment Dealers' Digest—see Appendix I).

9. Editors of *Fortune* Magazine. *Fortune's Guide to Personal Investing*. New York: McGraw Hill, 1963.

10. Engel, Louis. *How to Buy Stocks*. New York: Bantam Books, 1962.

11. Friend, I., and Vickers, D. "Portfolio Selection and Investment Performance," *Journal of Finance,* Volume 20, No. 3, September, 1965, pp. 391–413.

12. Furst, Sidney and Sherman, Milton. *Business Decisions That Changed Our Lives*. New York: Random House, 1964.

13. Graham, Benjamin, Dodd, David L., and Cottle, Sidney, with the collaboration of Charles Latham. *Security Analysis: Principles and Techniques*. New York: McGraw Hill, 1962.

14. Graham, Benjamin. *The Intelligent Investor*. New York: Harper & Row, 1965.

15. Hazard, John W., and Coit, Lew G. *The Kiplinger Book for Investing for the Years Ahead*. New York: Doubleday, 1962.

16. Hazard, John W., and Christie, Milton. *The Investment Business*. New York: Harper & Row, 1964.

17. Homer, Sidney. *A History of Interest Rates*. New Brunswick, New Jersey: Rutgers University Press, 1963.

18. Jacobs, Raymond H. and Kohn, Ezra. *Securities: What They Are; Their Markets Regulation; Analysis; Financial Planning*. Washing, D.C.: Kalb, Voorhis & Co., 1964.

19. Jenkins, David. *How to Build Capital and Income in Mutual Funds*. Larchmont, New York: Grosset & Dunlap, 1963.

20. *Management Investment Companies*. A monograph prepared for the Commission on Money and Credit by the Investment Company Institute. Englewood Cliffs, New Jersey: Prentice-Hall, 1962.

21. *Mutual Funds, a Statistical Summary, 1940–1963*. New York: Investment Company Institute.

22. Palance, Dean. *Mutual Funds: Legal Pickpockets?* New York: Vantage Press, 1963.

23. Person, Carl E. *The Save-by-Borrowing Techniques: Building Your Fortune, From Loan to Profit*. Garden City, New York: Doubleday, 1966.

24. Pope, Alan. *Financial Success for Salaried People*. New York: Vantage Press, 1966.

25. Pope, Alan. "Selecting Growth-Stock Mutual Funds by the Cash Flow/Performance Method." Alan Pope, 816 Val Verde Drive, SE, Albuquerque, New Mexico 87108.

26. *Public Policy Implications of Investment Company Growth*. Pre-

pared by the Securities and Exchange Commission, House Report Number 2337, 89th Congress, 2nd Session, 1966.

27. *Report of the Special Study of Securities Markets of the Securities and Exchange Commission.* House Document Number 95, Part 4, 88th Congress, 1st Session, 1963.
28. Rodda, William H., and Nelson, Edward A. *Managing Personal Finances.* Englewood Cliffs, New Jersey: Prentice-Hall, 1965.
29. Smith, Adam. (Pseudonym of George J. W. Goodman, editor, *Institutional Investor.*) *The Money Game.* New York: Random House, 1968.
30. Smith, Ralph Lee. *The Grim Truth About Mutual Funds.* Putnam, New York, 1963.
31. Straley, John A. *What About Mutual Funds?* New York: Harper & Row, 1967.
32. *The Money Managers.* Investment Company Institute. New York: McGraw Hill, 1967.
33. Unterman, Israel. *Creative Money Management for the Executive.* Garden City, New York: Doubleday, 1962.
34. Weissman, Rudolph. *Investment Made Easy.* New York: Harper & Row, 1962.

MAGAZINE ARTICLES

The following articles have been chosen for their general interest to mutual fund newcomers as well as to mutual fund shareholders.

1. "A New Look at Choices of the Mutual Funds," *U.S. News,* November 11, 1968. Explores the changes in fund portfolios and indicates the issues most heavily bought and sold by funds in the third quarter of 1968.
2. "About Face," *Forbes,* July 15, 1968. A brief but informative column on the entry of the life insurance companies into the mutual fund field and the difficulty of getting insurance salesmen fund-oriented.
3. "Avoiding Financial Pitfalls!" *The Air Line Pilot,* 1962. Raises crucial questions about the soundness of your financial program and contains helpful guidelines toward intelligent estate planning. Reprints available from Insurance Planning Corporation, 2934 Fulton Avenue, Sacramento, California 95821.
4. Cohn, Martin. "What Every Young Wife Should Know About Money," *Redbook,* September, 1968. Advice to young married women about purchases, savings and buying stocks and mutual funds, with a cautionary reminder that the small investor having no counsel is handicapped and must do her own research. Lists free publications and aid available to investors.
5. Davis, T. F., "NEA Mutual Fund," *NEA Journal,* November,

1964. Discusses a low-load mutual fund established for teachers.

6. "Give-ups Kick Back on Funds," *Business Week,* July 27, 1968. Discusses the SEC investigation into commission-splitting, and some of the industry's answers.

7. "Growth Funds Lose Their Glamor," *Fortune,* September 1, 1968. Discusses reversals in the performance pattern of some of the "go-go" funds.

8. "Have You Looked Into No-Load Mutual Funds?" *Changing Times,* February, 1965. No-load funds are explained and the reader is given some advice to follow before he invests in such a fund.

9. Hershman, A., "Will the Funds Run Companies?" *Dun's Review,* July, 1968. Considers the influence that the funds are exerting on the management of corporations, noting three major trends.

10. "Heyday of the Hedge Funds," *Dun's Review,* January, 1968. Discusses the controversial hedge fund, a highly speculative type of investment company, in terms of its methods, policies, and philosophy.

11. "How the Funds Are Dominating the Stock Market Now," *U.S. News,* April 17, 1967. Explains some of the factors of the impact of mutual funds on the stock market, an impact which is causing increasing concern both in Wall Street and Washington.

12. "How to Become a Millionaire," *U.S. News,* November 11, 1968. Indicates how an investment of $10,000 may grow to a million if an annual rate of 15% is realized on the investment.

13. "How to Turn Mutual Funds Into Income," *Changing Times,* August, 1965. An illustrated example of a mutual fund withdrawal plan.

14. "Investing: Longer-Range Outlook," *U.S. News,* November 11, 1968. Discusses the growing demand for stocks on the part of pension funds, mutual funds, life insurance companies, banks, individuals, and state and local governments.

15. "Investment Trusts and You," *Changing Times,* April, 1967. A clear explanation of open-end funds, no-load funds, closed-end funds, and leverage funds, their different goals and their special features, as well as some basic characteristics of all investment trusts.

16. "Investors Go to Sea," *Business Week,* August 31, 1968. Discusses mutual funds specializing in oceanography and considers the speculative nature of such stocks at this time.

17. "Keeping the Sales Pitch Blurry," *Business Week,* June 4, 1966. An informative article on the SEC's policy concerning television ads for the mutual funds.

18. Land, F., "What Every Young Father Should Know about Mutual

Funds," *Parents,* January, 1967. Some simple advice for the new investor in mutual funds. Describes accumulation method of purchasing funds.

19. "Life Insurance's Almighty Leap Into Equities," *Fortune,* October, 1968. Describes the enormous impact of the life insurance company entry into the mutual fund business.

20. Loomis, C. J., "SEC Has a Little List," *Fortune,* January, 1967. A critical appraisal of a number of the SEC proposals for modifying mutual fund operations, particularly load charges.

21. Loomis, C. J., "Two for the Price of One . . Dual-Purpose Fund," *Fortune,* February, 1967. A clear explanation of a new kind of mutual fund which simultaneously offers two different kinds of investors two different goals (income or capital gains).

22. Louis, A. M., "Those Go-Go Funds May Be Going Nowhere," *Fortune,* November, 1967. The "go-go" fever examined in detail through a discussion of the specific policies and philosophy of such funds.

23. Mayer, Milton, "Bernie Cornfield's First Billion," *Fortune,* March, 1968. The story of a financial genius who developed the world's largest mutual fund complex through daring innovation and American business techniques.

24. Murray, T. J., "Executives and Mutual Funds," *Dun's Review,* October, 1965. A concentrated guide to mutual funds as investments for the interested executive. Many types of funds and investment plans are given as well as cogent advice on evaluating funds.

25. "Mutual Fund Maverick: Sherman Dean Fund," *Business Week,* April 20, 1968. Tells the story of innovator Sherman Dean, manager of a mutual fund, who tried to manage his fund according to some of the SEC proposals in the light of its study of the fund industry.

26. "Mutual Funds: Pick With Care," *Changing Times,* February, 1963. Examines some of the main conclusions of the Wharton School Report, and their significance for a mutual fund investor.

27. "Mutual Funds Under Fire; Their Side of the Dispute," *U.S. News,* September 18, 1967. An interview with a leading mutual fund executive, giving the fund industry's views of the SEC proposals for changing mutual fund fees.

28. "Mutual Interest: Life Insurance Companies in the Mutual Fund Business," *Time,* January 19, 1968. Discusses the entry of life insurance companies into the mutual fund field, the number of such companies having doubled in 1968.

29. "Reader's Digest Fund," *Newsweek,* October 9, 1967. The story of the Digest's plans to sell mutual fund shares in West Germany.
30. Rosenfeld, M., "Investing in Mutual Funds," *New Republic,* July 2, 1966. Sets forth some basics about the purposes and the mechanics of mutual fund investing.
31. Rosenfeld, M., "Laying Down Some Rules for Mutual Funds." *New Republic,* January 7, 1967. A review of the SEC proposals on load charges in mutual funds.
32. "Rush to Swap," *Fortune,* May, 1965. "Swap," or exchange funds, are explained and their performance in the 1962 market slump is accounted for.
33. Seligman, D., and Wise, T. A., "New Forces in the Stock Market," *Fortune,* February, 1964. Examines the role and the influence of the big institutional investors on the stock market's performance.
34. "Stiffer Rules for Mutuals? Lower Costs to Investor," *U.S. News,* May 15, 1967. The SEC proposals on modifying load charges and the industry's reactions.
35. "Ten Most Misunderstood Facts about Mutual Funds," *Better Homes and Gardens,* May, 1968. A simple, clear article with some concrete suggestions about choosing a fund.
36. "The X-Factor and the High Flyers," *Fortune,* June 1, 1968. A fascinating article, with helpful chart, that contends that the extraordinary flow of new money into a fund can send the fund to a dizzying height but that the performance cannot last.
37. "Timely Ideas for Investors," *Changing Times,* November, 1966. Describes the differences between mutual funds and closed-end funds.
38. Treynor, J. L., "How to Rate the Management of Investment Funds," *Harvard Business Review,* January, 1965. Describes a simple, graphic method for evaluating fund performance and fund management, taking investment risk into consideration.
39. "Where Is the Big Money? Institutional Investors," *Time,* July 2, 1965. Points out the strong influence of the giant institutions in the stock market: insurance companies, pension funds, charitable foundations, and mutual funds.

Index

Index

Acquisition charge (*see* Sales charge)
Analysis form, 95–96
"Ask," 26

Balanced fund, 72, 75, 114, 151, 180, 184, 188
Barron's (pub.), 78
Bid, 26
Broker, 21, 34–35, 49, 60, 70, 86, 91–92, 95, 102, 168–69, 190, 195–96, 202
  commission to, 99
Brokerage allocation, 91–92
Business Decisions That Changed Our Lives (pub.), 193
Buying on margin, 80

Capital, 15, 37, 40, 49, 62, 71
Capital appreciation (*see* Growth)
Capital gain, 24–25
Capital gains, 32, 37, 41–42, 47–49, 67–69, 71, 74, 81, 83, 85, 88, 91, 94, 96–97, 102, 113, 121, 138, 150–53, 155–57, 160, 166, 168, 184–85, 194, 199

Capital Gains Research Bureau, Inc., 11
Capital preservation (*see* Stability)
"Closed-end" funds, 103–105
"Closed-end" investment companies, 23, 62, 75
"Closed-end" trust, 28
Contractual plan, 86–87, 137, (*see* also Front-end load funds)
  sales charge of, 137
Custodian bank, 108, 168–69
Custodian of fund, 87–88

Dividends, 24–25, 32, 35–37, 41–42, 47–49, 67–69, 71, 73–76, 81, 83, 85, 88–91, 94–96–97, 102, 113, 116, 119, 138, 150–53, 155–57, 166, 184–85, 192, 194
Dollar-cost average, 41
Dollar-cost averaging, 35, 71, 136, 141–43, 189
Dow Jones Industrial Average, 35, 51–52, 76, 180

Federal Securities Act of 1933, 170

219

Federal Securities Exchange Act of 1934, 171

Fixed return, 32, 38

Forbes magazine, 54, 58–60, 117, 121, 130, 133, 186, 190

Front-end load funds, 28–29, 87, 172, 198

FundScope (Pub.), 35, 45, 54–55, 58, 66–69, 72–73, 110–11, 114, 116, 138, 141, 186, 190–92

"Go-Go" funds, 119–133, 135, 164, 180, 182–83
   long-term capital gain of, 133
   long-term investing of, 131–32
   management personnel of, 123–24, 126
   philosophy of management, 126–127
   portfolio policies of, 124–26
   redemption fees of, 132–33
   sales commissions of, 132–33
   short-term gains of, 132

Government bonds, 32–33

Growth funds, 41–46, 49–51, 72–75, 81, 112–115, 147–49, 157, 186–187

Growth-income fund, 72, 75

Growth of investment, 40, 55, 70–72, 79, 93, 110–11, 121, 135, 141–142, 160, 184, 186–93

Huxley, T. H., 125

Income funds, 71–75, 83, 114, 148–149, 151, 157–60, 188–89, 192

Income of investment, 40, 46, 55, 79, 111, 115–19, 135, 141–42, 148, 190, 197

"Income only" funds, 49–50, 74

Income tax, 35, 49, 89–90, 138, 151, 153, 161, 166, 168

Investment Companies (pub.), 60, 62, 186, 190

Investment Company Act of 1933, 28

Investment Company Act of 1940, 27, 100, 106, 163, 168, 171, 178

Investment Company Charts (pub.), 64, 186, 190

Investment Company Institute, 165, 167, 194

Investment
   funds, 36
   goal and policy, 79–80
   plans, 95
   restrictions, 80
   risk, 34, 79
   trusts, 26–27

Keogh Act, 36, 91

Letter of intent, 86

Load charge, 25, 29, 60, 198

Load funds, 25, 107–19, 128, 132

Long-range growth, 79

Long-term appreciation of capital, 81

Long-term capital gain, 90, 133

Long-term investments, 39, 49, 65, 71, 106, 119, 131–32, 134–35, 138, 198

Long-term rising markets, 141

Management, 34, 39, 43, 46, 50, 79, 80, 91–93, 103, 115, 122–23, 165

Management fee, 24–25, 29, 51, 103, 108–109, 118, 169, 172–83, 198

National Association of Securities Dealers, 29, 100, 103, 162–64, 166–67, 195, 203
Net asset value per share, 23–24, 47–49, 76, 78, 81, 85, 87, 89, 93–94, 96, 98, 108, 118, 121, 128, 152–53, 157, 164, 167, 194
New York Stock Exchange, 52–53, 87, 100, 105, 167, 202
New York Stock Exchange Composite Index, 51
New York Times, The, 78
No-load funds, 25–26, 103, 107–19, 128, 130, 195

Open account plan, 87
Open-end funds, 117
Open-end investment company, 23
Open-end trust, 28
Over-the-counter market, 23
Over-the-counter stocks, 102

Package of funds, 71, 149
Performance funds (see "Go-Go" funds)
Performance record of funds, 81, 112–16, 122, 129, 142–43, 165, 167, 169, 187, 193, 198–99
Portfolio, 23–25, 34, 50, 71, 78–79, 91, 94, 103, 106, 115, 118
Price stability, 40, 111, 135, 190
Prospectus, 28, 46–47, 73, 75, 77–98, 142, 162, 167–68, 185, 191, 194–95
Financial statement of, 93

Purpose of fund, 79

Rate of decline, 35, 51
Rate of return, 37, 48
Redemption fee, 88, 109, 111, 113, 132–33, 138
Right of accumulation, 86

Sales charge, 28–30, 32, 62, 73, 86, 92, 97, 99, 107–110, 113–18, 135, 137–38, 142, 164, 168
Sales commission, 99, 104–105, 108, 113, 132
San Francisco Examiner, 99
Securities and Exchange Commission, 16–17, 27–30, 47–48, 73, 77, 87, 100, 103–106, 128, 161, 163, 166–69, 171, 173, 177–78, 180–81, 195, 198–99
Short selling, 80
Short-term capital gains, 199
Short-term investing, 49, 119, 132
Short-term performance, 64, 117
Short-term results, 72
Short-term success, 121
Stability of investment, 49–51, 55, 75, 79, 114–15, 121, 141–42, 184–85, 188–89
Standard & Poor's Corp., 52–53, 59
Standard & Poor's 500 Stock Average, 51, 59
Standard & Poor's Index, 60

Underwriter, 92, 99, 106, 108, 179
U. S. Senate Banking Committee, 29, 99–100
University of Pennsylvania Law School, 122

Volatility, 23
Voluntary plan, 87, 137
Voting rights, 95

Wall Street Journal, The, 78
Wharton Report, 100, 110, 174–75, 180

Wharton School of Finance, 100, 110, 113–14
Wiesenberger Services of Nuveen Corp., Arthur, 54

Yield, 46–48, 72, 115, 121
Yield/income, 47–49